About The Author

Robert Hughes

Robert Hughes is a certified public accountant licensed in California and Texas. He has owned and operated a private CPA practice since 1981 and has over 25 years of experience as a micro-business owner. Prior to beginning his own practice, he served as the chief business officer of a single campus university.

In his CPA practice, Hughes focuses on serving self-employed individuals and micro-businesses. He offers a full range of tax-related services—from preparation of individual and business tax returns to tax planning and IRS examinations. Hughes also provides consulting in the areas of financial strategies, business formations and modeling, as well as acquisitions and expansions. In addition, he offers consultations on computer systems design, installation and implementation.

Since 1986, Hughes has served on the board of directors for the National Association for the Self-Employed. He is currently president of the association, a position he held from 1991 to 1993 and from 2001 to the present.

His positions as a CPA and as president of the NASE give Hughes a unique perspective on the intricate business and tax issues faced by self-employed individuals and micro-business owners. He sees firsthand the challenges they face compiling information for and filing tax forms, meeting tax compliance requirements of complex federal and state laws, and staying up to date with tax law changes.

Hughes brings his technical knowledge as a CPA, his insight as a small-business owner and his experience as president of the NASE to this book in the hopes that you will find new strategies that will simplify your taxes.

About The NASE

The National Association For The Self-Employed (NASE)

The National Association for the Self-Employed (NASE) is the nation's leading resource for the self-employed and micro-businesses. The association helps remove financial and knowledge hurdles to starting and growing a micro-business. It does so by delivering a broad range of benefits to help entrepreneurs succeed and to drive the continued growth of this vital segment of the American economy.

Since its founding in 1981, the NASE has championed the interests of micro-businesses and provided an array of business, financial and personal benefits that lower the everyday costs for self-employed individuals.

Today the NASE represents more than 600,000 people, including members and their dependents. The association actively advocates for micro-business issues in Washington, D.C., with a strong legislative agenda that includes seeking tax equality in health care, tax relief, retirement security, Social Security reform and support for federal small-business programs.

The association serves its members by bringing big-business benefits to the micro-business community. Members receive significant discounts on a variety of useful benefits—from tax resources and health insurance to business supplies and financial products.

How to Contact the NASE

To find out more about the NASE or to join the association, use these contacts:

- Online: www.NASE.org
- By Telephone: 800-232-NASE
- By Mail: P.O. Box 612067, DFW Airport, Texas 75261

INTRODUCTION

I see it everyday. A self-employed consultant with a file full of questions about which expenses are deductible on Schedule C. A bakery owner who's about to be audited by the IRS for incorrectly categorizing and deducting business expenses on Schedule C. A graphic artist who doesn't understand depreciation of business equipment. A freelance sales representative who could have saved a bundle of money with just a little advance tax planning before the end of the year.

These are creative, intelligent, motivated sole proprietors. They start businesses, play by the rules, maybe hire a few employees and then find themselves bewildered by the financial demands and complexity of income taxes.

That's why I wrote this book.

As a certified public accountant and as president of the National Association for the Self-Employed (NASE), I know the challenges and obstacles faced by micro-business owners and self-employed individuals. I also understand the tax issues and inequalities they encounter in the course of building their businesses. And I think these business owners deserve some straightforward answers, especially when it comes to preparing and filing their income tax returns.

That's what this book is all about. It's designed to help sole proprietors understand their tax liabilities and to help them prepare their tax returns. Micro-business owners and entrepreneurs don't have the luxury of putting high-powered tax accountants on staff to figure out confusing and complex tax laws. By walking through Schedule C—line-by-line—this book helps sole proproprietors get a better grasp of business expenses and how to report those expenses so that they are categorized properly. Correctly reported business expenses reduce the risk of examination by the IRS.

If you're a sole proprietor responsible for filing Schedule C, this book helps you accurately categorize your business expenses and report them on each line. But this book can do much more for you.

You can use it to plan your tax strategies early in each year. By knowing which business expenses will be deductible, you can estimate your tax liability and find ways to reduce your taxes. Using this book and Schedule C may even help you find new deductions you weren't aware of—deductions that will put real dollars in your pocket.

You can also use this book in conjunction with Schedule C to organize your bookkeeping and record keeping. I included a pocket on the back cover so that you can keep receipts and tax documents handy. Whether you use computer software or a paper ledger to track expenses, you can set up your record keeping to reflect each line on Schedule C. At the end of the year, you simply fill out Schedule C using your records that match the schedule line-for-line. For ease, many of the tax forms mentioned in this book are included in the back. You can tear them out, fill them in, and mail to the IRS.

This book covers the most common scenarios for filling out Schedule C. It answers basic questions and gives guidance for each line. However, it doesn't delve into every intricacy of the tax code.

And it can't replace the knowledgeable advice you can get from a tax professional who understands your unique business transactions. If you have a complex tax issue—or even a simple one that you don't fully understand—talk to your tax professional, because your facts and circumstances are critical to tax planning and filing. Don't depend upon this book for all your answers. Get accurate advice that applies specifically to your business situation.

I hope this book gives you information and knowledge you can use to build a stronger business. I hope it takes some of the frustration out of handling your tax responsibilities as a sole proprietor. I hope you find it useful in running your business.

TABLE OF CONTENTS

ABOUT SCHEDULE C

Before we wade into the actual line-by-line explanations of Schedule C, there are a few general rules you need to know.

Business expenses

When the IRS refers to business expenses, it's talking about the operating costs of running your business. These are costs that exclude expenses you have to capitalize or the costs of goods sold.

To be deductible on Schedule C, a business expense must be an ordinary and necessary cost of operating your business. An ordinary expense is one that is common and accepted in your industry or your trade. A necessary expense is one that's appropriate and useful for your industry or your trade.

Categorizing business expenses

As you'll see, properly categorizing each of your business expenses and reporting them on the appropriate of line of Schedule C isn't always an easy task. There are gray areas.

But it is critically important to understand as much as you can about properly categorizing business expenses—and to report them correctly. If you don't report your expenses on the proper line, you can raise unnecessary questions about the deductibility of the expense.

Receipts and record keeping

If the IRS elects to review your business tax return, you will have to defend your categorization of expenses. You could also be asked to show that expenses were ordinary and necessary to your business. And you could be told to produce the actual receipts for the expenses you deduct.

For those reasons, it's crucial that you maintain good financial records for your business. That means keeping business and personal expenses—as well as business and personal bank accounts—separate. It means getting receipts for expenses and filing them for future reference. It means taking the time to keep your financial books in order.

The more written documentation you maintain for your business finances, the better. These can include:

- Calendars that show time, place, date and purpose of business meetings
- Diaries or logs to note expenses that aren't accompanied by a receipt, such as parking and tips
- Mileage logs that show where, when, why and how far you drove for business purposes
- Written leases and contracts pertaining to your business
- Copies of tax forms you file
- Correspondence with local, state or federal agencies
- Paid invoices from suppliers and contractors
- Copies of invoices and sales receipts you provide to customers
- Deposits slips and statements from your bank
- Business licenses

And the list goes on. If in doubt about a piece of paper related to your business—keep it. The records could come in handy when you're filling out Schedule C, and certainly when the IRS asks for information associated with your business and your business tax return.

Who should file Schedule C?

Whether or not you file Schedule C depends upon your type of business entity. The chart below shows the different types of business entities along with the corresponding forms that should be filed.

BUSINESS ENTITY	FORM TO USE
Sole Proprietor	Form 1040 Schedule C
C Corporation	Form 1120
S Corporation	Form 1120S
Partnership	Form 1065
Limited Liability Company	
Electing corporation status	Form 1120
Electing partnership status with 2 or more members	Form 1165
Single member electing *sole proprietorship status*	Form 1040 Schedule C
Husband-wife business jointly owned and operated *other than operated as a corporation*	Form 1065
Self-employed person	File *based* on business entity
Statutory employee	Form 1040 Schedule C
Minister	Form 1040 Schedule C
Farmer	Form 1040 Schedule F
Income from non-business activity	Form 1040 Line 21

COMPLETING SCHEDULE C

Here is an approach to completing your Schedule C that will save you some time and a few headaches.

1. Get a blank copy of the Schedule C to keep in front of you. You can download a copy directly from the IRS Web site at www.irs.gov. There is also a tear-out copy of Schedule C in this book.

2. Use a pencil when completing the first copy and have an eraser close by.

3. Keep this book and a copy of the IRS instructions to the Schedule C at hand.

4. Fill in lines A through H first before you start with the numbers.

5. If you have inventories, fill in Part III, Cost of Goods Sold, on page 2.

6. Complete Part IV, Information on your Vehicle, on page 2.

7. Calculate your vehicle expense using both available methods – the standard mileage rate method and the actual expense method – in order to determine which option will provide you the largest deduction.

8. Fill in line 9, Car and truck expenses.

9. Complete Form 4562, Depreciation and Amortization. A tear out of Form 4562 is included in this book.

10. Fill in line 13, Depreciation and section 179 expense.

11. Fill in all other required income and expense lines, using this book and the IRS Schedule C instructions along the way.

12. Fill in line 29, Tentative profit (loss).

13. Complete Form 8829, Business use of Your Home, if you have an office in your home. A tear-out of Form 8829 is included in this book, as well as a line by line guide.

14. Complete line 30, Expenses for business use of your home with the information from the Form 8829 above.

15. Fill in line 31, Net profit or (loss). If you have a loss, go back and recalculate Form 4562 if you claimed a section 179 expense and the Form 8829 since some items are limited based on the earnings from the business.

GETTING STARTED

Lines A through H

These lines identify your business and your accounting methods.

Name of proprietor

Enter your name here, not the name under which you conduct your business.

For example, if your name is John Smith, and your business name is John Smith Consulting, don't put John Smith Consulting on this line. Put only your name, John Smith, on this line. Even if your business does not have a name, or if the name of your business is simply John Smith, still put only your name on this line.

If you and your spouse jointly own and operate the business, don't put both names on this line. In fact, you shouldn't even use Schedule C. You should prepare and file Form 1065, U.S. Partnership Return of Income.

If you are a single member of a limited liability company, don't use the name of the limited liability company. Instead put only your name.

Social Security number (SSN)

Put your Social Security number in this space. The Social Security number requested in this space relates to the "Name of Proprietor" discussed above. Regardless of the entity form in which you operate your business, use the Social Security number for the name of the proprietor.

Report the Social Security number of the sole proprietor even if your business has an employer ID number (EIN).

LINE A

Principal business or profession, including product or service

On this line describe your business or professional activity that you conduct to earn money. If your business does several things, then determine which activity within your business is the "principal" or "primary" source of your income.

Let's say you have a courier service. You bill customers for those services. But in addition you provide specialized packing and crates for shipments. You also bill customers for that service. If the courier service part of the business generates the higher income of the two, then report on this line, "courier services for other businesses," rather than "packing and crating services for other businesses."

 Caution: If you operate more than one business, you must file a Schedule C for each unrelated business entity. Use a separate Schedule C for each business for which you have a business license, bank account, fictitious business name or which you view to be a separate business.

LINE B

Enter code from pages C-7, C-8 & C-9

This box is primarily for statistical data collection information for the IRS. The pages "C-7, 8 & 9" refer to the instructions for Schedule C. These pages contain a listing of the standardized North American Industry Classification System (NAICS). There are instructions on those pages to assist you in determining which NAICS code you should use for your business.

Simply review the list and select the code that best describes what your business does.

Above, I used the example of the delivery service. The NAICS code from page C-8 would be 492000 "Couriers and Messengers." Even though your courier service provides packaging and crating, your primary business is courier services. Use the NAICS code that best matches your primary business.

LINE C

Business name

If your business doesn't have a name, leave this line blank. If you operate under your name only (the same name you used on the "Name of proprietor" line), then don't put your name here. On this line put only your business name if you have a name for your business other than your own.

LINE D

Employer ID number (EIN)

If your business has an EIN, report it on this line. If you don't have an EIN, leave this box blank.

Your business may not have an EIN. An EIN is a nine-digit number assigned by the IRS. To receive an EIN, you must you complete and file Form SS-4.

The IRS requires that you have an EIN if you have employees. You also need an EIN if you're required to file a separate excise, estate, trust, or alcohol, tobacco, and firearms tax return.

You might also need an EIN if you open a business checking account in a business name other than your own.

 Caution: Don't put your Social Security number in this box. If you don't have an EIN, leave the box blank.

LINE E

Business address

If you operate your business from your home, it's not necessary to put your home address on this line.

If your business address is other than your home address, write your business address on this line. Use a street number (a physical address) rather than a mail box number. The IRS wants to know where you operate your business, not just where you get your mail.

LINE F

Accounting method

On this line simply check the box that describes the accounting method you use in your business.

The majority of businesses use either the cash or accrual method of accounting, but some specialized industries use accounting methods specific to their trade.

For example, a construction contractor may use the cash or accrual method of accounting, but also use "percentage of completion." The contractor should check box 3 "Other," and write in "percentage of completion" on the line.

Cash accounting

If you use the cash method of accounting, you generally report income when you receive payment and record expenses when you actually pay the bill.

Here's an example. Jill, a graphic artist, uses the cash method of accounting. She designs a brochure for Bob's Truck Repair. Jill delivers the brochure and sends Bob a bill for $500. Jill only includes the $500 in income when she actually gets the money from Bob. Also, for her business Jill buys paper supplies from ABC Papers. ABC sends Jill an invoice for her purchases. Jill only takes an expense deduction when she actually pays the ABC invoice.

Accrual accounting

If you use the accrual method of accounting, you report income as you earn it. Regardless of when you actually receive the money from customers you billed, you still report the income as you earn it.

Likewise, you record expense deduction when you incur the expenses, regardless of when you actually pay for them.

Here's an example. Joe, an architect, uses the accrual method of accounting. He drafts house plans for his client Marsha. Joe delivers the house plans and his bill to Marsha. He reports his fee as income when the job is done, even if he hasn't received the money yet.

Caution: If you have questions about which accounting method your business uses or should use, contact a business accounting and tax professional for advice. Also be aware that changing accounting methods from the one you now use to a different one requires approval from the IRS.

LINE G

Did you materially participate in the operation of this business?

This line seems simple because it requires a straightforward "Yes" or "No" answer. However, the answer has far reaching implications as to the deductibility of losses and credits that your business may incur.

A discussion of material participation goes well beyond the scope of this line-by-line guide to completing Schedule C.

To correctly answer line G, research the material participation and passive activity loss rules on page C-2 & C-3 in the instructions for Schedule C. You should read the instructions to fully understand how they apply in your specific circumstances. Also, you should strongly consider the advice of a tax professional to assist you in answering this question.

LINE H

If you started or acquired this business in the current year

If you started the operations of the business listed on line A during this year, check the box. If you operated the business in the prior year, leave the box blank.

The day you open your doors is the day that your business starts. For instance, in October 2003, you began researching and preparing to start your own business. But you didn't actually open your doors until January 2004. In that case, your started your business in January 2004, and you would therefore check the box on Line H.

PART I: INCOME

This part of the Schedule C calculates your gross income from your trade or business. Any income you derive from your trade or business is reported in this part of the Schedule C.

Most business income is from the sale of products or services. In most instances, you will receive income in the form of cash, checks, electronic funds transfer, credit card payments and debit card payments. But even if you receive no cash and instead receive goods or services in exchange for your services or products, you still have gross income that must be reported in Part I.

Barter Income

Bartering is simply the exchange of goods or services. You must report barter income as part of your gross receipts in the same manner as other income.

For example, you are a house painter and you paint your accountant's house. In exchange your accountant creates a business plan for you. The value of the business plan is the amount of barter income you received for painting your accountant's house. On line 1 of Part 1, you must report the barter income that you have received.

In addition, you and the accountant should exchange Forms 1099-B, Proceeds from Broker and Barter Exchange Transactions, to show the value of the barter arrangement. Form 1099-B may be obtained by calling 800-829-3676.

More than one business

If you operate more than one business, you must complete a separate Schedule C for each business. Be sure that the income reported on each Schedule C pertains to that trade or business.

Items NOT reported in Part I

These items are not reported as gross income in Part I:

- Loans for any purpose or from any source.

- Appreciation in the value of any property you own. Appreciation is taxable when you sell or otherwise dispose of your property.

- Certain exchanges of like-kind property. Sometimes called "tax-free or tax-deferred exchanges", these transaction have specific conditions that must be met. Consult with your tax professional before entering into property exchanges.

- Consignment of your products given to others to sell. If you have products or merchandise on consignment, you don't report the income until the merchandise is actually sold.

- If you sell business assets, such as equipment, building or land, the income your business derives is reported on other schedules in your tax return.

LINE 1

Gross receipts or sales

Total all of the income you have received for the sale of your goods or service. Enter that amount on line 1.

You may receive Form 1099-MISC from your customers. In box 7 of Form 1099 is the total amount that a customer paid to your during the current year. Include that amount on line 1, gross receipts or sales.

If you didn't receive a 1099-MISC, but derived income from the sale of goods or service, include that amount on line 1. The key is that even if you did not receive a form 1099-MISC, you still must include the income that you received.

If you received barter income, include that amount on line 1.

The box on line 1 is for statutory employees. Statutory employees are full-time life insurance agents, commission drivers, traveling salespersons and certain home workers. If you receive a Form W-2, and the "Statutory employee" is checked in box 13, you are a statutory employee. On line 1 you must report the statutory income shown in box 1 of Form W-2. Be sure you also check the box on line 1.

 Caution: If you received income from your trade or business and income as a statutory employee, you must file two Schedule Cs.

LINE 2

Returns and Allowances

Some businesses account for returns of merchandise separately so that they can track information about sales. If you included returns and allowances on line 1, "Gross income," then you can exclude returns and allowances on line 2.

Here's an example. Sherry buys your merchandise with the understanding that it can be returned for a full or partial refund. Sherry returns the merchandise, and you give her a full refund. If you include the original sale amount on line 1, then report the refund amount on line 2.

LINE 3

Subtract line 2 from line 1. This total represents your net sales. This is a good place to stop and check your math, before going further.

LINE 4

Cost of goods sold

On this line, enter the amount from Part III, Cost of Goods Sold, line 42. You can find it on page 2 of Schedule C. For instructions about calculating your cost of goods sold, see Part III of this book.

If your business doesn't produce merchandise for sale or doesn't buy and resell merchandise, then you will not have any amount to report on this line.

LINE 5

Gross Profit

Subtract line 4 from line 3. This total represents your gross profit.

Gross profit is your total gross income minus returns and allowances on line 2 and cost of goods sold on line 4.

You can use this amount to assess whether your gross receipts, returns and allowances, and cost for goods sold are reasonably accurate. Here is an example. You expect to make a 25 percent profit on the sales of your merchandise. When you divide line 5 (gross profit) by line 1 (gross sales), the result is 48 percent. The result should be about the same as you expected for your percent of profit, in this example 25 percent. But your calculations show your gross profit at 48 percent. This means you could have made an error in your reported gross income or cost of good sold. Check your math to make sure that you are not over or under reporting your income.

LINE 6

Other Income

On this line report other types of income you received from your trade or business. Don't include on this line any income from the sales of your product or services.

Items of income to include here:

- Interest on business cash, such as checking or savings accounts.

- Interest on business investment accounts (but no retirement accounts).

- Bad debts that you deducted in a previous year, but for which you received money this year. There are called "Bad debt recoveries" and should be reported here.

- Prizes and awards in connection with your business. For example, your business entered a raffle through the chamber of commerce and won a $500 gift certificate. Report the $500 on line 6.

LINE 7

Gross Income

Add lines 5 and 6. Again, this is a good place to check your math.

Note that this line is called "Gross Income", and line 1 is called "Gross Receipts." If you operate a service business and don't have any cost of goods sold or other income, these two lines may show the same amount. Generally, however, line 1 and line 7 will be different amounts.

PART II: EXPENSES

LINE 8

Advertising

At first glance, line 8, "Advertising," looks like one of the easiest to decipher on Schedule C. But be careful. You probably have more advertising expenses than you realize—and they must all be included here.

When calculating your expenses for line 8, think of advertising in broad strokes. Include on this line all of your costs for marketing, promoting, publicizing and advertising your business.

Broadcast & print advertising

Let's start with the most obvious deductions for this line: traditional forms of advertising. On line 8, include the cost of running ads on radio or television. Also deduct the cost of placing ads on billboards or in newspapers, magazines and newsletters. This includes trade publications and association newsletters, such as the local chamber of commerce newsletter.

In addition to placement costs, advertising production costs are included on this line. For instance, if you pay a graphic designer to create your ad, deduct the fee on line 8. The same is true for a copywriter. If you hire an advertising agency to produce broadcast or print ads for your business, the full cost is included on this line. Perhaps you design, write and produce ads on your computer. But you hire an advertising consultant to give you advice about where to place the ads. In that case, deduct the fee you pay to the consultant as an advertising expense.

The cost of classified advertising—whether to promote your business or find employees—is also deducted on line 8.

Costs you incur to produce printed flyers are deducted on line 8. That includes printing, graphic design, copywriting and other production expenses. The flyers may be given to customers, posted on bulletin boards around your city, distributed to neighborhood businesses or homes, or mailed. If you mail the flyers, the postage cost is not included on line 8, but on line 48, "Other expenses." If you pay an independent contractor to deliver your flyers, that expense is included on line 10, "Commissions and fees," not on line 8.

Expenses for advertising in the yellow pages or the white pages are included on line 8. If you pay to list your business in a trade group or association directory, that cost is also deductible on line 8. Some chambers of commerce and business associations produce city maps that show the location of businesses. If you pay to be included on the map, that's an advertising expense as well. Take the deduction on line 8.

Many micro-businesses support the local community by purchasing ad space in annual calendars that are produced by nonprofit organizations then sold as fund-raisers. Some businesses also buy ad space in programs that accompany a nonprofit's fund-raising event. If your business participates in either of these, the amount you pay for advertising is deductible on line 8.

Signage

The costs of signs that promote your business are also advertising expenses and deducted on line 8. This includes signs placed inside or outside of your business.

 Caution: The costs for signs that are more permanent in nature and that will benefit your business for more than one year aren't deductible on line 8. These expenses are capitalized and recognized as expense through depreciation on line 13, "Depreciation and section 179 expense deduction."

Let's say you own a restaurant. You produce table-top tent cards to announce the daily dinner special. The costs of those cards are considered advertising expenses.

The same is true for a retail shop. You create sale cards that are displayed on shelves, racks or merchandise. The cards are advertising. Deduct their costs on line 8.

If your retail business purchases shopping bags imprinted with your business logo or name, deduct the cost of the bags and the printing on line 8. However, if you buy generic shopping bags that don't advertise your business, then you deduct the cost of the bags on line 22, "Supplies."

Other signage costs that are deducted on line 8 include:

- Magnetic vehicle signs
- Painted signs on vehicles
- Outdoor directional signs that help customers locate your business
- Painted signs on exterior windows or building walls
- Indoor or outdoor banners that advertise your business

Online advertising

If you pay to promote your business on the Internet, those expenses are deductible as advertising costs on line 8. Here are a few of the most common costs:

- Banner ads
- Ads in e-magazines
- Ads run on another Web site
- Ads placed in e-newsletters (other than one produced by your business)
- Fees paid for listings on search engines

In addition, if you pay someone to design, update, write and host a Web site for your business, these costs are deductible on line 8. Expenses for tracking hits and generating traffic reports are also deductible advertising expenses.

E-mail marketing is also considered an advertising expense. Fees you pay to contractors for designing, producing, writing and generating e-mail marketing campaigns are deducted on line 8. If you purchase lists of names for your campaign, that expense is deductible too.

Newsletters

Many micro-business owners use printed and electronic newsletters to keep in touch with clients, announce new products and services, report industry trends, and distribute customer surveys. If your business publishes a newsletter—online or offline—you deduct most of the expenses on line 8. All production costs of newsletters are reported on line 8: graphic design and artwork, copywriting, proofreading, printing or fees for electronic distribution.

However, if you mail or ship a printed newsletter, the postage or shipping costs are reported on line 48, "Other expenses."

Some self-employed professionals purchase pre-printed newsletters from industry associations. The newsletters are personalized by imprinting the professional's business name and contact information on the pre-printed newsletter. The cost of purchasing such a newsletter is deductible as an advertising expense on line 8.

Marketing materials

Marketing materials consist of brochures, videos, CD-ROMs, Rolodex cards, direct mail pieces, price lists you give to customers and a host of other items printed with your contact information. All of the expenses required to create and produce these materials are deductible on line 8. You can also deduct the cost of purchasing mail lists of prospective customers.

Beware that the costs for mailing or shipping marketing materials are not deducted on line 8. They're included on line 48, "Other expenses."

 Caution: Letterhead, envelopes and business cards are not considered marketing materials, and expenses for these items are not included on line 8. Instead, costs for these materials are deducted on line 18, "Office Expense."

Public relations

All of the expenses related to PR for your business are deducted on line 8. These include:

- Developing and printing press kits
- Writing and distributing press releases
- Photographs of products, your office or building, employees, owners and customers that are used for PR purposes

- Writing and placement of articles in publications
- Costs associated with public relations events, such as press conferences
- Fees you pay to PR professionals for working with the media on your behalf

Although print publications generally don't charge a fee for running your press release, the same isn't true for companies that distribute press releases electronically. These companies almost always charge a fee—and you can deduct it on line 8.

In addition, if you provide product samples to the media for review, deduct your actual cost of the product (not its retail value) on line 8. Of course this only applies if you allow the media to keep your product. If the product is returned to you, you don't get a deduction.

Promotions

There are as many ways of promoting your business as there are sole proprietors. Regardless of the methods you use, the deductible expenses for promotions go on line 8.

For instance, if you host a grand opening gala to introduce prospective customers to your new enterprise, all of the related expenses are included on line 8—catering, a live band, decorations, signage and the list goes on.

Beware. Throwing a big holiday bash doesn't count as a promotion. And the expenses you incur aren't deductible on line 8. However, the party counts as an entertainment expense if the event meets these requirements:

❏ The attendees are existing or prospective customers

❏ You discuss business at the party

❏ You have a reasonable expectation of generating a business benefit from the event

If your event meets those requirements, then you can deduct 50 percent of the expense on line 24b, "Travel, meals, and entertainment."

On a smaller scale, you may purchase key chains (or pens or magnets or mouse pads) imprinted with the name of your business. If you give these promotion items to clients and prospective customers, the costs are fully deductible, even if you don't give them all away.

If you mail or ship the giveaway items, however, the shipping or mailing costs are deducted on line 48, "Other expenses."

 Caution: You may at times purchase giveaway items that aren't imprinted with the name of your business. Books, candy and fruit baskets fit this example. In this case, the items are considered gifts, not promotional items. As gifts, the costs are limited to $25 per year per recipient and are deducted on line 48, "Other expenses."

Trade shows

Maybe you set up a booth at a local career fair in hopes of attracting employees. Or maybe you travel across country to show your products at an industry trade show. Either way, most of your expenses are deductible on line 8.

These include the cost of producing the actual booth that you use as well as the cost of transporting the booth. It includes the fees you pay to display your booth at the show—from the space and drapery rentals to carpenters and electricians. It also includes any number of ancillary items you need to rent or buy—name tags, special equipment, a listing in the trade show directory and so on.

However, your expenses for travel to and from the trade show and your accommodations during the show aren't deducted on line 8. They're included on line 24, "Travel, meals, and entertainment."

The same is true when you hire additional personnel to work the booth. That expense doesn't go on line 8. If you hire workers and pay a pre-determined wage, include that cost on line 26, "Wages." If you hire sales people who earn a commission on the products they sell while at the show, report those commission expenses on line 10, "Commissions and fees."

Other advertising expenses

Sole proprietors are shrewd at finding innovative ways to advertise and promote their businesses. So it's impossible to list every conceivable advertising expense. But here are a few more examples of expenses that are deducted on line 8:

- T-shirts or uniforms imprinted with the name of your business for the local peewee volleyball team
- Marketing materials designed for faxing to customers and prospective clients
- Posters promoting your business

- Promotion items for vehicles, such as sunshades imprinted with the name of your business
- Desk and wall calendars imprinted with your business information

LINE 9

Car and Truck Expenses

If you use a car or truck in business you can deduct the operating and maintenance costs on line 9. But be careful. This line of Schedule C is highly abused and subject to close scrutiny by the IRS.

On line 9, deduct all automobile expenses related to your business. This includes driving to a client's office, to the office supply store, to the post office, to multiple job sites, etc. It also includes driving for out of town business trips.

If you're a claiming a deduction on line 9 you must also complete either:

- Part IV, Information on Your Vehicle, on page 2 of Schedule C
or
- Form 4562, Depreciation and Amortization

Completing one of these before you tackle line 9 will help you figure your deduction for line 9. See the instructions later in this book for help completing Schedule C, Part IV, or Form 4562.

Methods of deducting expenses

There are two methods for figuring your car and truck expenses: standard mileage rate and actual expenses. You can generally choose to use the method that gives you the largest deduction.

You can switch between using the standard mileage rate and actual expenses from year to year to get the largest deduction—but only if you use the standard mileage method the first year you place the vehicle in service for your business. If you use the actual expense method the first year, you must use that method for the entire time you use that vehicle for business purposes.

Caution: Regardless of which method you use, you must have documentation to support the deduction. That generally means keeping a detailed log to support your business use of the vehicle. Mileage estimates aren't acceptable to the IRS. If you use the actual expense method, you should also keep receipts to substantiate all of the car expenses.

If you lease a car or truck that you use for business purposes, you can still take a deduction for operating expenses on line 9. You can use either the standard mileage rate or actual expenses.

Standard mileage rate

This method is the easiest to use. Each year the IRS sets a standard mileage rate. Simply multiply the number of business miles you drive by the mileage rate in effect for the current year.

The rate for 2002 was 36.5 cents per mile and for 2003 is was 36 cents per mile. For 2004, the rate was increased to 37.5 cents per mile.

Here's an example of using the standard mileage rate. Assume you drove 10,000 business miles during 2004. The mileage rate for 2004 was 37.5 cents per mile. Multiply 10,000 miles by .375 cents. Your total car expense deduction is $3,750.

Caution: The standard mileage rate changes every year. In some years, the IRS has even set two different rates within the same year. You can find the current year's mileage rate in the Schedule C instructions under line 9, on page C-3 & C-4.

If you use the standard mileage rate, you can't deduct any of the actual expenses you incur for operating or maintaining your car. However, parking and tolls can be deducted in addition to the standard mileage rate.

Caution: If you want to use the standard mileage rate for a car you lease, you must use that method for the entire time you lease that car. You can't change to the actual expense method even if it gives you a larger deduction.

Actual expenses

This method of calculating car expenses is more difficult than using the standard mileage rate. But, in a year when you have high repair and maintenance costs, you might get a larger deduction by using this method.

If you use the actual expenses method, you simply add up all of the operating and maintenance costs you incurred for the car during the current year. Operating and maintenance costs include:

- Gas and oil
- License and registration fees
- Insurance

- Garage rent
- Tires
- Minor and major repairs
- Maintenance items such as oil changes and tire rotations
- Interest you pay on the car or truck loan
- Car washes and detailing

If you use your car solely for business purposes and never for commuting or personal purposes, it's easy to figure your actual expenses. Just add up all of your costs and report the total on line 9.

If you use your car for personal as well as business purposes, you must allocate your expenses between personal use and business use. Here's the step-by-step process for allocating expenses:

- First complete Part IV on page 2 of Schedule C (or Form 4562 for depreciation). This will show you how many total miles you drove during the year. It will also show you how many miles you drove for business, personal purposes and commuting.

- Divide the number of business miles you drove by the total miles you drove for the entire year. The result is your percentage of business use.

- Multiply your total actual expenses by the business percentage. The result is your car expense deduction.

After you figure your car expense deduction, add any parking or toll fees you paid. Then report the total on line 9.

Here's an example. You drove a total of 20,000 miles during the year. Of that 20,000, you drove 15,000 miles for business purposes. Divide 15,000 (business miles) by 20,000 (total miles). The result is 75 percent. Your total actual expenses for the year were $4,000. Multiply $4,000 by .75 (your business usage). The result is $3,000. You paid $25 in parking and toll fees for the year. Add that $25 to your $3,000 car expense. Report the total, $3,025 on line 9.

 Caution: Don't include any depreciation expense in your actual expenses. Your depreciation is calculated on line 13.

 Caution: There are complex rules to determine if 100 percent of your auto lease payments can be deducted. See IRS *Publication 463, Travel, Entertainment, Gift and Car Expenses*, for more information.

Use of more than one vehicle

If you drive more than one vehicle for business purposes during the year (other than a fleet), include the total expenses for all of the vehicles on line 9.

Here's an example. You drive a truck to different construction job sites. You use the standard mileage rate to figure your deduction for the truck. You drive a car when visiting clients or running business errands. You use the actual expense method to figure your deduction for the car. Add the deduction for your truck and your deduction for your car. Report the total on line 9.

Fleet operations

According to IRS rules, you operate a fleet of vehicles if you use five or more vehicles *simultaneously* in your business.

If you operate a fleet, you cannot use the standard mileage rate to figure your expense deduction on line 9. This applies even if one of the vehicles is your personal car used exclusively by you. If you operate a fleet, you must use the actual expenses method to figure your expense deduction on line 9.

Here's an example. Sally has a courier service. She uses six cars in her business. The cars are used simultaneously by Sally and her employees. Sally must use the actual expense method to figure her expense deduction on line 9 for all of her cars.

Other expenses deductible on line 9

The costs listed here are deductible on line 9 if you incur them in the course of doing business. To report these expenses, simply add them to your car deduction and enter the total on line 9.

- Parking fees (other than garage rent if you use the actual expenses method)
- Toll fees
- Transit fares (buses, subways, taxis, etc.) you incur for local transportation. If you incur any of these expenses while on a business trip away from home, report the costs on line 24, "Travel, meals, and entertainment," otherwise, include those items on line 9.

Expenses *NOT* deductible on line 9

- Commuting expenses—the costs of traveling from your home to your office or from your home to a customer's place of business.
- Miles you drive for personal purposes.
- If you fly to a destination for a business purpose and then rent a car, that expense is not deductible on line 9. Instead, report that expense on line 24, "Travel, meals, entertainment.
- If you must rent an automobile for a short time to replace the car you normally use for business, that expense is not deductible on line 9. Instead, report that cost in Part V, "Other expenses."

Here's an example. You normally use your personal car for business purposes. When your car breaks down, you take it to your mechanic for repairs. The repairs take a week to complete. During that week, you rent a car. You use the car for both business and personal purposes. Calculate the business miles you drive during the week and divide that number by the total miles you put on the rental car. This gives you the business percentage use of the rental car. Multiply the total cost you pay for the rental car by the business use percentage. Enter the total in Part V, "Other expenses."

For more information

For more help on figuring your car and truck expenses, see IRS *Publication 463, Travel, Entertainment, Gift and Car Expenses.*

LINE 10

Commissions and Fees

On this line deduct commissions and fees you pay to non-employees to produce revenue for your business.

This can include commissions you pay to independent sales representatives who sell your products or services. It can also include commissions you pay to someone who prospects for your business or a finder's fee you pay for business that someone outside of your company brings in.

For example, Brian is a bookkeeper. He contracts with an independent telemarketer to find potential clients who might need his bookkeeping services. For each prospect that is converted to a client, Brian pays the telemarketer a commission, which is a percentage of the client's annual billing. This commission is deductible on line 10.

Here's another example. Beth sells collectible dolls. She rents a booth in a local antique mall. In addition to paying rent for her booth, she pays the mall a 5 percent commission of her total monthly sales. Beth deducts the commissions on line 10. However, she deducts her rental payments on line 20b, "Rent or lease of other business property."

Or take this example. John is a sculptor. He pays his agent a 15 percent commission of the total price each time the agent sells one of his sculptures. John deducts those commissions on line 10.

 Caution: Commissions you pay to employees are reported on line 26, "Wages." Employees can be compensated in many ways, including hourly wages, bonuses, salary, by production and commissions. Even if you compensate employees on a commission-only basis, don't deduct that expense on this line. Report that amount on line 26, "Wages." Only report on line 10 the commissions you pay to non-employees who produce revenue for your business.

Business investments

You can also deduct on line 10 fees you pay in association with business investment activities. Fees for opening, closing or transferring business investment accounts are also deductible.

 Caution: Brokerage fees for the buying or selling of stocks, bonds, and mutual funds are not deductible on line 10. Those fees are considered part of the purchase price (in the case of a buy) and a reduction of the sale price (in the case of a sale). Those brokerage fees are part of the purchase price and sale price of securities transactions as reported on Schedule D, Gains and Losses.

 Caution: Don't include on line 10 fees associated with any retirement, pension or profit-sharing accounts, either business or personal. Also don't include fees you incur in your personal, non-retirement investment accounts.

Other fees deductible on line 10

Fees for credit reports on customers, suppliers, employees, yourself as a business owner and your business are deductible on line 10.

Fees NOT deductible on line 10

- Fees you pay to independent contractors, unless the fees are commissions or finder's fees you pay to produce revenue, as discussed above. Other fees you pay to independent contractors are reported in the category of expense for which the contractor's services are provided. For instance, fees to an advertising consultant are deductible on line 8, "Advertising." Fees for a contractor to repair your printer are deducted on line 21, "Repairs and maintenance."

- Fees you pay for attorneys, tax preparers and other professionals. Those are deducted on line 17, "Legal and professional services."

- Wages, bonuses and commissions you pay to employees. Those expenses are deducted on line 26, "Wages."

- Fees for Internet use. Those are deducted on line 18, "Office expense."

- Fees you pay to city, state or federal governments for business licenses. Those are deducted on line 23, "Taxes and licenses."

- Shipping and delivery fees. Report those in the category of expense for which the fees were used. For instance, if you ship your computer to the manufacturer for repairs, report that shipping fee on line 21, "Repairs and maintenance." If the shipping and delivery fess are in connection with inventory or products you ship, those fees are deducted on line 39 as part of your cost of goods sold. If the fee doesn't fall in a specific expense category, report it on line 18, "Office expense."

- Fees you pay to attend business-related seminars, workshops and conferences. Those are considered educational expenses and are reported on line 48, "Other expenses."

- If you work in a home office, don't deduct homeowner association fees on line 10. Those will be included on line 30, "Expenses for business use of your home," if you take the home office deduction.

LINE 11

Contract Labor

On this line include all payments that you made to independent contractors for services that were provided to your business. If the services were provided in direct connection with the production of your merchandise, do not include those items on line 11. Instead those payments for services would be included as cost of goods sold in Part III of the Schedule C.

Also do not include payments made to your employees in the form of salaries or wages. Wages paid to employees would be included on line 26.

 Caution: The classification of an individual providing services to your business as an independent contractor or as an employee is not a matter of choice. The specific facts and circumstances of the relationship will dictate whether the worker is an employee or an independent contractor. Unfortunately, the lines between employee and independent contractor are not all that clear. Here are some guidelines that the IRS uses when trying to distinguish employee status. The key point is that the classification is not one of choice, but is based on the facts of the situation.

An individual performing services is an employee if the person for whom the services are performed has the right to control and direct them in the details and means by which the services are performed. The worker is an independent contractor if the person for whom the services are performed has the right to control and direct him only as to the result to be accomplished. Independent contractors typically include physicians, lawyers, dentists, veterinarians, contractors, subcontractors, public stenographers, auctioneers and others who engage in an independent trade, business or profession in which they offer their services to the public. As a general rule, this means that the individual has other clients beside you. In this case the payments would be reported on line 11.

The determination of whether an individual is an employee or an independent contractor is based on the facts and circumstances surrounding the employment arrangements. Factors to be considered include the right to direct the performance, the right to discharge the worker, and the provision of tools of the trade or a workplace by the person for whom services are provided. If these factors are present, the person performing the services is treated as an employee even if he is designated as a partner, coadventurer, agent, independent contractor or any other title. The person for whom services are performed has control over the performance of the services if he has the right to direct them and to enforce compliance with his instructions, even if no instructions are actually given. Thus, an employer has control over employees who work without receiving instructions because they are either highly proficient or conscientious. In these cases the payments would not be reported on line 11, but would be included on line 26, "Wages."

This can be confusing and is often a tough concept to nail down. The IRS uses form SS-8 to determine employee or independent contractor status. The form consists of three pages of questions, both objective and subjective. You can download the SS-8 form from the IRS Web site at www.irs.gov and review the list of question to see how the IRS might view your situation. Even if you do not file the form asking for an IRS determination, it will give you a good idea of the types of things they look at.

LINE 12

Depletion

A deduction is allowed for the use of natural resources when that use is in connection with your trade or business. If your business involves mining, maintenance of wells, natural gas, timberlands, etc, the production of income related to that business uses those natural resources. The IRS recognizes that those resources are being used up and therefore, a deduction for that use is included on line 12 of the Schedule C.

Key points to keep in mind in claiming the deduction for depletion are that you must have an economic interest in the property, and your goal for the extraction of the natural resources is to make money.

The deduction is similar to the deduction for depreciation that would be included on line 13. The basic method for calculating the amount of the deduction is called "cost depletion" since the deduction is based on the adjusted cost or basis in the property, which is also similar to depreciation. Another method is called the percentage depletion method and is available for all depletable property except for timber.

As you might guess, the calculation of the depletion deduction can be quite complicated, and it applies to only a small number of small-business owners who file a Schedule C. If your business includes the use of natural resources that will allow you to take advantage of a depletion deduction, the best advice here is to make sure you visit with your personal tax advisors about your specific facts and circumstances to maximize your allowance deduction.

LINE 13

Depreciation and Section 179 Expense Deduction

When you purchase property to use in your business, you generally can't take a business deduction for the full cost in the year you acquire the property. Instead you must usually deduct the cost over a period of years. By deducting a part of the cost each year, you eventually get business expense deductions for the entire cost. That's what depreciation is all about.

There is an alternative to depreciating business property. It's known as the "section 179 expense deduction." This special tax provision allows you the option of claiming a deduction for the entire cost of a qualifying business asset in the first year the asset is placed in service. There are limits and restrictions on this option, which we'll talk about later.

Form 4562, Depreciation and Amortization

To claim depreciation or a section 179 expense deduction on line 13, you must complete and file Form 4562, Depreciation and Amortization. You can use the Form found in the back of this book.

Your depreciation deductions from Form 4562 will be carried over to line 13 on Schedule C.

Who must file Form 4562

You must file Form 4562, Depreciation and Amortization, if you meet any of these tests:

- You are claiming depreciation on business property you purchased and placed in service during the current year
- You are claiming depreciation on a vehicle or other listed property
- You are claiming a section 179 expense deduction

You don't have to file Form 4562 if you are claiming continued depreciation on property that's not considered "listed." Also, if you are claiming automobile expenses based on the standard mileage rate (as opposed to actual expenses), you don't have to file Form 4562.

 Caution: Don't combine depreciation expenses for more than one business on the same Form 4562. If you operate more than one business, use a separate Form 4562 to claim depreciation or a section 179 expense deduction for each business.

Listed property

Certain types of business properties are considered "listed property." Listed property is subject to special depreciation rules. Listed property includes:

- Cell phones
- Vehicles under 6,000 pounds
- Computers and peripheral equipment, such as printers and monitors—unless these are used at a regular business office, including an office that qualifies for a home office deduction.

Other property that can be depreciated

You can depreciate business property on Form 4562 if it meets these requirements:

- Property that you own
- Must be used in your trade or business
- Must have a useful life of more than one year
- Must be property that wears out, gets used up or becomes obsolete

Here are some examples of business property that you can depreciate:

- Production machinery and equipment
- Office equipment, such as copiers
- Tools
- Telephone equipment
- Vehicles
- Computer software (except anti-virus software)
- Furniture and fixtures

Property that cannot be depreciated

Certain types of property can't be depreciated. Examples include:

- Property put into service and disposed of within the same year
- Inventory
- Land
- Repairs and replacements to property that don't increase the value of the property, make it more useful or lengthen its useful life

Section 179 expense deduction

This tax provision gives you the option of claiming a deduction for the entire cost of qualifying business assets in the first year that you place them in service. Even if you elect to use section 179, you must still complete Form 4562, Depreciation and Amortization.

The section 179 expense deduction is a bonanza for small-business owners. If you qualify for section 179, you get a handsome deduction that significantly reduces your income taxes expenses for the year.

To qualify for the section 179 expense deduction, the property must meet these requirements:

- ❑ It must be tangible personal property that you actively use in your business or trade, for which a depreciation deduction would be allowed.
- ❑ It must be newly purchased property that you didn't previously own.
- ❑ It must be used more than 50 percent in your business.

Certain types of property *don't* qualify for section 179 expense deduction. These include:

- Property you acquire by inheritance or gift
- Property you acquire from another business that you own

There are limits and restrictions to section 179. For instance, in 2004 the maximum deduction is $102,000 (as shown on line 1 of Form 4562). To fully understand section 179, read IRS *Publication 946, How To Depreciate Property*.

Completing Form 4562

Form 4562 is complex and detailed. Before completing the form, it's helpful to read IRS *Publication 946, How To Depreciate Property.*

Here, I'll outline the best approach to filling out Form 4562:

- Part V: Complete this section first. It relates to vehicles and other listed property.
- Part I: Complete this section second. This will help you calculate your section 179 expense deduction.
- Part II: Complete this section next if you placed new property (other than listed property or cars) into service during the current year.
- Part III: Complete this section if you have depreciation for any property that was placed in service before the current year.
- Part IV: Complete this section last. It totals your depreciation deductions. Line 22 on Form 4562 provides the total depreciation deduction you can take for the current year. Transfer the amount from Form 4562, line 22 to Schedule C, line 13.
- Part VI: This part relates to your amortization deductions, not your depreciation deductions. Any amortization deductions you have in this section are carried over to your Schedule C, Part V, "Other expenses."

LINE 14

Employee Benefit Programs

Deductions on line 14 include the cost of employee benefit programs that you provide to your employees and the families of your employees.

Benefit costs to include on line 14

The most common employee benefits include:

- Employee and employee's dependent's health insurance
- Accident insurance related to employees
- Group term life insurance
- Dependent care assistance programs
- Benefits paid under a Medical Reimbursement Plan
- Employer provided educational assistance

There are certain limits and restrictions on some employee benefits, depending on your type of business. For example, health insurance premiums paid for the business owner would not be included on this line. Rather, those premiums are to be included on line 31 of page 1 of form 1040. And there are maximum limits per employee on the amount of education assistance that can be provided. If your business qualifies for these types of employee benefits, include the costs on line 14.

For more information, see these IRS publications:

- *Publication 15, Circular E, Employer's Tax Guide*
- *Publication 15-A, Employer's Supplemental Tax Guide*
- *Publication 15-B, Employer's Tax Guide To Fringe Benefits*

Expenses *NOT* deducted on line 14

- Expenses associated with employee pension and profit-sharing plans, including SEPs, SIMPLEs, IRAs, and annuities. Deduct those costs on line 19.

- Amounts you pay for your own benefits, such as health insurance or retirement plan contributions. These amounts may still be deductible, but are not included on Schedule C. Health insurance premiums you pay for your own coverage are included on Form 1040, line 31. Retirement contributions you make on your own behalf are reported on your Form 1040, line 32.

- Leased vehicles and other leased property that you allow employees or service providers to use. Deduct that expense on line 20, "Rent or lease."

- Other property that you own and allow employees or service providers to use. Report that expense on line 13 as a section 179 or depreciation deduction. For instance you buy a billiards table for use in the employee lounge. Don't deduct the expense of the table as an employee benefit. Report the cost on line 13.

- On-site employee facilities. Maybe your business provides on-site childcare or an on-site gym. The expenses associated with these facilities are not deducted on line 14. Instead, you report the costs of operating the facilities in the appropriate category. For instance, wages for personnel to oversee the child care facility or gym are reported on line 26. Equipment expenses for the facilities are reported on 13. The cost of utilities is reported on line 25.

- Personal use of business equipment, such as computers, printers and fax machines. The cost of the equipment is reported on line 13.

- Nominal secretarial services, such as typing personal letters. You may allow employees to occasionally use the services of secretaries or administrative assistants for personal matters. However, you deduct the wages of the secretaries and assistants on line 26.

- Nominal legal services provided to your employees by your business attorney. This might include reviewing lease agreements or offering consultations. Although you may provide this as a fringe benefit, the costs you incur are reported on line 17, "Legal and professional services."

LINE 15

Insurance

On this line, deduct the premiums you pay for insurance policies that protect your business. Of course, there are exceptions and requirements you must meet, as listed later in this chapter.

Common insurance deductions on line 15

Here's a list of the most common types of insurance expenses that are deductible on line 15:

- Fire, theft, flood and other property and casualty insurance (note the home office exception later in this chapter)
- Merchandise and inventory insurance
- Credit insurance that covers losses from unpaid debts
- Malpractice insurance that covers your personal liability for professional negligence
- Professional liability insurance
- General liability insurance for your place of business
- Business interruption insurance that covers loss of profits if your business must shut down because fire, flood or other causes
- Errors and omissions insurance
- Business overhead insurance that pays overhead expenses during your disability

- Employee performance bonds that insure faithful performance by your employees

For example, doctors and dentists can deduct the cost of medical malpractice insurance. If your office is in a flood plain, you can deduct the cost of business interruption insurance that would cover your loss of profits if a flood wiped out your business. Perhaps you install carpet for living and are worried that someone will trip on the carpet and suffer injury. In that case, you could acquire liability insurance and deduct the expense on line 15.

Workers' compensation insurance

Workers' compensation insurance that is required by state law is usually deductible on line 15. Even if your state has optional workers' compensation insurance requirements, you can deduct the expense on this line.

Some companies won't do business with self-employed individuals unless they carry workers' compensation insurance for themselves. If you must pay for workers' compensation in order to establish or continue a working relationship, the premiums are deductible on line 15.

For instance, a self-employed logger worked on a timber company's land. The company required the logger to acquire workers' compensation before renewing his contract. Since the insurance was required for the logger to continue his business, the cost of premiums was an ordinary and necessary business expense.

Insurance prepayments

At times, you may purchase a policy that covers more than the current year. In that case, you deduct only the portion of the premium that covers the current year. This holds true even if you use the cash method of accounting.

For example, you purchase an insurance policy in July 2004 and pay the full annual premium of $1,200. The policy coverage extends from July 2004 through June 2005. That premium payment covers the last six months of 2004 and the first six months of 2005. For 2004, you deduct only $600 on line 15 (six months of coverage in 2004). You'll deduct the remainder of the premium ($600) on your 2005 tax form.

Insurance expenses NOT deductible on line 15:

- Health insurance, group term life insurance or accident insurance that you provide to your employees. Report those deductions on line 14, "Employee benefit programs."

- Health insurance for yourself. Report these premiums on Form 1040, page 1, as "self-employed health insurance deduction."

- Homeowner's insurance. If you work from a home office, the portion of your homeowner's insurance that applies to your home office is deducted on line 30, "Expenses for business use of your home."

- Automobile insurance. If you use actual expenses to calculate the cost of using your vehicle in your business, the insurance premiums you pay are reported on line 9, "Car and truck expenses." If you use the standard mileage rate to figure your automobile expenses, you can't deduct any vehicle insurance premiums.

- Disability insurance for yourself that covers loss of earnings because of sickness or injury.

- Any portion of insurance premiums reported in Part III, "Cost of Goods Sold."

- State unemployment insurance. Report that as a separate expense on line 48, "Other expenses."

- Contributions to federal unemployment taxes (FUTA). Report that as a separate expense on line 48, "Other expenses."

- Insurance to secure a loan.

- Amounts credited to a reserve you set up for self-insurance.

LINES 16a and 16b

Interest

On these lines deduct all of the interest you pay during the tax year on debts related to your business. These debts can be in the form of business loans, lines of credit, mortgages on business property, credit cards, home equity loans and loans that are part business and part personal.

If you use money from a loan of any kind to pay for a business expense, then the interest relates to your business. You must meet all of the following requirements to be eligible to deduct the interest on a business debt:

- ❏ You are legally liable for that debt.
- ❏ You and the lender intend that the debt be repaid.
- ❏ You and the lender have a true debtor-creditor relationship.

When you get a loan from a financial institution, it's easy to prove the debtor-creditor relationship. The paperwork required to establish the loan spells out the relationship with payment terms, interest rates, due dates and provisions for non-payment.

Many sole proprietors tap other sources for loans, including family and friends, suppliers, business associates, even customers. These are certainly legitimate loan sources and should not be overlooked in deducting business interest. Just be sure you have the proper written documentation to prove the debtor-creditor relationship.

Mortgage interest (other than a principal residence)

Interest that you pay related to a mortgage on real property (other than your main home) used in your business is included on line 16a.

When you pay mortgage interest during the year, you generally receive a Form 1098 from the lender. If you receive a Form 1098, enter that interest amount on line 16a.

If you don't receive a Form 1098, you report the interest on line 16b. For instance, let's say you and another person own the business property together, and the other person receives the Form 1098. On line 16b, enter the share of the interest you pay and attach a statement to your return showing the name and address of the person who received the Form 1098. In the left margin next to line 16b, write "See attached."

There is an exception to this rule. Let's say you own the property with your spouse, and you file your taxes jointly, and your spouse receives the Form 1098. In that case, you enter the mortgage interest on line 16a.

Home mortgage interest

In general, if you use your main home to secure a loan, the interest may be deducted in one of several different places on your tax return: if you itemize deductions, on Schedule A; if you claim the home office deduction, Form 8829 and Schedule C; or on Schedule C as a business.

The interest is usually deductible as qualified home mortgage interest, however, if the proceeds are used in your trade or business that portion of interest can be deducted here.

Business lines of credit

Business lines of credit give you access to continued borrowing. You establish a line of credit with a lender, and then borrow the money, as you need it to pay business expenses.

Interest that you pay for lines of credit is deductible on line 16b as long as the borrowed funds are used for business purposes.

Credit card interest

If you carry balances on credit cards used exclusively for business purposes, you can deduct all of the annual interest on line 16b.

If you carry balances on credits cards that are used for personal and business purposes, you must allocate the interest appropriately. That means you determine how much of the interest you incurred for personal purchases and how much you incurred for business purchases. Only the interest charged for business purposes can be deducted on line 16b.

Interest from home equity lines of credit

If you secure a line of credit using the equity in your home, and commit all of the funds to financing your business, the interest you pay is deductible on line 16b.

However, if you use the part of the funds to finance your business and part for personal expenses, then you must allocate the interest you pay between the two uses. Only the interest you pay on the business part of the loan is deductible on line 16b.

Loans that are part business and part personal

If you use proceeds from a loan partly for business expenses and partly for personal expenses, you must divide the interest between the two. Only the interest you pay on the business part of the loan is deductible on Schedule C, lines 16a and 16b.

For instance, you take out a loan for $100,000. You use $20,000 (20 percent of the loan) for a personal vacation. You use $80,000 (80 percent of the loan) to renovate your office building. Only 80 percent of the interest you pay is allocated to business and deductible as a business expense on line 16b. The other 20 percent is personal interest expense.

When you repay any part of a loan that's allocated to business and personal use, as in the example above, treat it as being paid in the following order:

1. Personal use
2. Business use

This repayment schedule could impact the amount of interest that's deductible as a business expense. It could also impact when you can take the business interest deduction. To keep things simple, it's best to separate business loans from personal loans.

Allocating loan interest

You must allocate (classify) interest expense so that it's deducted on the correct line of your return. In general you classify the interest you pay the same way you classify the loan proceeds. If proceeds from a loan are used to pay for business expenses, then the interest on the loan is deductible as a business expense.

For example, you acquire a $10,000 bank loan. You deposit the money in your business banking account and use the funds to pay business bills. All of the interest you pay on the loan is a deductible interest expense. Report it on line 16b.

Another example. You acquire a $10,000 secured bank loan. You use your vintage Model T automobile, a personal asset, to secure the loan. But you spend the $10,000 to remodel your office. Even though the loan was secured with a personal asset, the proceeds of the loan were used for a business expense. Therefore, the interest you pay on the loan is a deductible business expense. Report it on line 16b.

Here's another example. You acquire a $20,000 secured loan to help pay for your child's college education. You secure the loan with property used in your business. Even though the loan was secured with a business asset, the proceeds from the loan were used for a personal expense. Therefore, the interest you pay on the loan is not a deductible business expense.

When to deduct interest expenses

Whether you use the cash method of accounting or accrual method determines when you actually deduct interest expenses.

- Cash method: Generally you deduct only interest that you actually pay during the tax year that applies to that tax year. If you pay interest that applies to a future tax year, you can only deduct that part that applies to the current tax year.

- Accrual method: You deduct only interest that accrues during the tax year, regardless of whether you actually paid the tax. Don't deduct any interest you pay before the year it's due.

Other interest deductions on line 16b

- If you're charged interest because of late payments of employment taxes, that interest is deductible on line 16b.

- If you're responsible for part of a business debt, you deduct on line 16b only your share of the total interest paid.

- If you pay off a mortgage early and incur a prepayment penalty, the penalty is considered interest. You can deduct it on line 16b.

Interest *NOT* deductible on lines 16a or 16b:

- Interest you pay on personal loans.

- Mortgage interest if you have a home office. The portion of your home mortgage interest that applies to your home office is deducted on Form 8829, "Expenses for the Business Use of Your Home." For a detailed discussion of the home office deduction and Form 8829, see Line 30 in this book.

- Interest you pay on debts that are related to investment property are not included on lines 16a or 16b.

- Penalties you pay for late or underestimated tax payments.

- Expenses to obtain a mortgage on business or income-producing property. Costs such as mortgage commissions, recording fees and abstract fees are considered capital expenses and are added to the cost basis of the property. You can't deduct these expenses on lines 16a or 16b.

- If you have a debt that is used to pay for the production of real or tangible property, you must usually capitalize the interest. Capitalized interest is treated as a cost of the property produced. It's not deductible on lines 16a or 16b.

For more information

To find out more about deducting interest on lines 16a and 16b, see these IRS publications, which can be found on www.irs.gov:

- *Publication 535, Business Expenses*
- *Publication 550, Investment Income & Expense*
- *Publication 936, Home Mortgage Interest Deduction*
- *Publication 537, Installment Sales*

LINE 17

Legal and Professional Services

Legal and professional fees that are ordinary and necessary expenses directly related to operating your **business** are deductible as business expenses on line 17. Don't deduct on line 17 legal and professional expenses related to your non-business or personal affairs.

Don't deduct on line 17 legal and other professional fees you pay to acquire business assets, such as property or equipment. You add those expenses to the cost basis of the asset.

Also, if you incur legal and professional costs before you actually start your business, you must capitalize those expenses rather than report them on line 17.

Business startup expenses are those expenses you incur before you actually begin your business operations. They can include the following items:

- Analysis or survey of potential markets, products, labor supply, transportation facilities, etc.
- Advertisements for the opening of the business
- Salaries and wages for employees who are being trained and their instructors
- Travel and other necessary costs for securing prospective distributors, suppliers and customers
- Salaries and fees for executives and consultants, or for similar professional services such as lawyers and accountants used to create business plans, business entities, accounting systems, etc.

Business startup expenses are not deductible, but rather are capitalized and amortized over at least 60 months beginning on the date you begin to operate your business.

Legal services

Sooner or later, legal advice is crucial to sole proprietors. It can get expensive. But the costs are deductible on line 17. Here are a few examples of services attorneys provide—and expenses you can deduct:

- Filing for and reviewing patents, trademarks and copyrights
- Preparing and reviewing contracts
- Collecting business debts
- Resolving business disputes
- Consulting on employment issues
- Representing you (as a business owner) and your business in legal matters

The expenses you incur to handle legal services for personal affairs are not deductible. For example, if you use an attorney to draw up an estate plan, the portion of the fee that is connected to your business is deductible. However, the portion of the fee related to your will is not deductible because that portion is a personal expense, not a business expense.

Another example is the legal cost you incur for collecting a bad debt. Unless the debt was created as part of your business (a customer that did not pay his bill) the legal fees are not deductible. If you make a loan to a friend, even though you paid the money from your business, the loan is not considered a business loan, and therefore any legal fees incurred to collect the money are not deductible.

Tax services

Tax services are provided by a variety of professionals:
- Individual tax preparers, such as CPAs, accountants and enrolled agents
- Tax attorneys
- Companies, such as H&R Block, Jackson Hewitt and Commerce Clearing House
- Direct costs for preparing and procession your tax return online

Most of the costs you incur for tax services are deductible on line 17. Some examples:

- Preparing tax returns for your business

- Consulting on business tax matters

- Representing of you (as a business owner) and your business with the IRS or in tax court

If a tax professional prepares your complete tax return, only the fees you pay for preparation and filing of Schedule C and its related forms are deductible as business expenses. The other fees you pay for preparation of your personal return may be deducted on Schedule A if you itemize deductions.

Other professional services

Fees you pay to independent contractors should generally be deducted in the categories for which they provide services. For instance, if you pay a consultant for advice about advertising, include that expense on line 8, "Advertising." If you hire an office organizer to clean up files and clutter, report that cost on line 18, "Office expense."

Professional service expenses that you don't report on other lines of Schedule C can be deducted on line 17. Here are a few examples:

- Bookkeeping and payroll services.

- Research assistance. For instance writers, video producers and filmmakers often hire independent contractors to research projects. You might also hire someone to research competitors or competitive products.

- Virtual assistant. This is someone who maintains his or her own office and works as an independent contractor for your business. Virtual assistants may write business letters, obtain pricing for office equipment, proofread business documents, make travel arrangements for your business trips, etc. You may pay the assistant hourly, by the project or on retainer. All of the fees are deductible on this line.

- Business coach. Business coaches can help you set goals and create new strategies for your business. Fees for the services are deducted on line 17.

- Protocol expert. Perhaps you're doing business with a company in a foreign country. You need to know the protocols for business meetings, introductions, business dinners, etc. You hire a protocol expert to provide answers. That fee is deductible as a professional service expense.

LINE 18

Office Expense

This line is not as obvious as it first appears. Most office expenses, such as supplies, utilities, furniture and rent are deducted on other lines on Schedule C. So what expenses do you report on line 18? Here are a few examples:

- Maintenance services for living or artificial plants and fish aquariums. If you lease those items and maintenance is included in the lease cost, then report the full expense on line 20b.
- Janitorial services for your office and cleaning of individual items, such as rugs or draperies.
- Coffee or bottled water services
- Telephone answering service, except voice mail service that's included as part of your telephone service.
- Inexpensive items for office décor, such as posters, candles and flower arrangements. Purchases of depreciable art are not deductible on line 18. They must be capitalized and recognized as an expense through depreciation, which is then reported on line 13. If you lease artwork for your office, deduct that expense on line 20b, "Rent for other business property."
- Signs you must display in your office or building to meet local, state or federal regulations, such as safety or licensing signs.
- Window washing services
- Lawn maintenance around an office building used solely for business.

Expenses NOT deductible on line 18:

- Furniture and fixtures. These items must be capitalized and recognized as an expense through depreciation, which is then reported on line 13, "Depreciation and section 179 expenses."
- Home office expenses. Report those on Form 8829, "Expenses for Business Use of Your Home."
- Office rent. Deduct that on line 20b, "Rent for other business property."
- Leasing costs of office equipment, such as computers and copiers. Report those on line 20a.
- Utilities for your office. Report those on line 25, "Utilities."

- Significant office renovations. These expenses are capitalized and recognized as expense through depreciation, which is be reported on line 13, "Depreciation and section 179 expenses."

LINE 19

Pension and Profit-Sharing Plans

If you make contributions on behalf of your employees to certain retirement plans, you can deduct the contributions on line 19.

These types of plans are included:

- Matching Contributions to 401(k) Plans
- SEP (Simplified Employee Pension)
- SIMPLE (Savings Incentive Match Plan for Employees)
- Qualified plans, such as a Keogh
- Annuity
- Profit-sharing pension
- Stock bonus pension

Amounts that you contribute to a plan on your own behalf are NOT deducted on line 19. They're reported on Form 1040, line 32 "Self-Employed SEP, SIMPLE and qualified plans."

When to deduct contributions

For SEP IRA or SIMPLE IRA plans, you can deduct contributions you make for each tax year if they are made by the due date of your federal income tax return for that year. The due date includes extensions for filing your return.

For example, you're a sole proprietor operating on a calendar tax year. Your tax year ends on Dec. 31, 2004. You file your federal income tax return on April 15, 2005. You can make SEP IRA and SIMPLE IRA contributions for 2004 up until April 15, 2005, when you file your return. The retirement contributions you make in 2005 (for 2004) are deductible on your 2004 tax return provided that indeed are made by the due date of the return.

Retirement plan fees

You can also deduct on line 19 any administrative or trustees' fees that you incur to maintain a retirement plan for your employees.

Tax credits

You may qualify for a tax credit if you initiate a retirement plan for yourself or your employees in the years 2002 through 2004.

Employers with less than 100 employees can receive a tax credit for establishing new retirement plans. The credit equals 50 percent of the startup costs you incur to create or maintain a new employee retirement plan. The credit is limited to $500 in any tax year and is included on Form 3800, General Business Credit.

For more information

See these IRS publications for more information about retirement plan contributions and deductions:

- *Publication 535, Business Expenses*
- *Publication 560, Retirement Plans for Small Business*
- *Publication 590, Individual Retirement Arrangements*

LINE 20

Rent or Lease

Rent is considered any amount you pay for the business use of property you don't own. However, not all rent or lease payments are deductible on line 20. See the list below of rent and related items that are not deductible on line 20—even though they may be deductible elsewhere on Schedule C.

On line 20a, you generally report payments you made to rent or lease:

- Vehicles
- Machinery
- Equipment (including office equipment such as computers and copiers)

On line 20b, you generally report your rent or lease payments for other business property, such as office space, land, retail space and buildings.

Vehicles

How you deduct lease expenses for a vehicle depends upon whether you use actual expenses or take the standard mileage rate when figuring business use of your vehicle.

For instance, if you lease a car and you use the standard mileage rate for the entire term of the lease, then don't report any lease expenses on line 20a. Instead, you simply report your standard mileage rate deduction on line 9.

But let's say you lease a car and you deduct actual expenses. In that case, here's how you report the business use expenses of the car:

- On line 20a, report your business portion of costs for gas, oil, repairs, insurance, tires, license plates, and lease payments etc.

Caution: You must deduct the actual expenses of operating your leased vehicle if:

- You use your leased vehicle for hire (such as a taxi)

or

- You use more than one vehicle simultaneously in your business (such as in a fleet operation)

If you are reporting lease payments on line 20b and if you lease the vehicle for 30 days or more, your deduction on line 20b may be reduced by an "inclusion amount." The lease inclusion amount, for practical purposes, limits the amount of the lease deduction based on the fair market value of the vehicle. If the value of your business vehicle is greater than $12,800, you may have an inclusion amount, which means that you will not be able to deduct all of your lease payments, even if you use your vehicle 100 percent for business. To calculate your inclusion amount, see IRS *Publication 463, Travel, Entertainment, Gift, and Car Expenses.*

If you rent a vehicle in conjunction with a business trip, don't deduct that cost on line 20a. Instead, report that expense on line 24, "Travel, meals and entertainment."

Other rent or lease deductions

On line 20 you can deduct the amount you pay to cancel a business lease. Simply add the expense to your lease costs and report them on the appropriate line (20a or 20b).

You can also deduct on line 20 any non-refundable deposits you must make to acquire the lease.

On line 20 you can also deduct any taxes you have to pay to the landlord or to government taxing agencies. However, when you deduct those taxes depends upon the accounting method you use.

If you use the cash method of accounting, deduct the taxes as additional rent in the year in which you pay them.

If you use the accrual method of accounting, deduct the taxes in the year in which all of the following occur:

❑ You have responsibility for paying the taxes on the leased property.

❑ You know how much the taxes are.

❑ You actually use the property.

Capitalizing rent expenses

Under certain circumstances, you must capitalize rent expenses rather than deducting them on line 20. In general, if you produce property used in your business or if you produce property for sale to customers you must capitalize rent expenses.

For example, you rent construction equipment to build a storage facility for your business. The rent you pay for the equipment must be capitalized as part of the cost of the storage facility.

Another example. You make children's toys. You lease a building to house your raw materials and production equipment. The rent you pay on the building is not deductible on line 20a. Instead, you must report the rent expense on line 4, "Cost of goods sold."

Expenses NOT deductible on line 20:

- If you rent a house or apartment and use part of it for a home office, the rent would not be included on line 20. However, you may be able to deduct a portion of the rent under the home office deduction included on line 30.

- If you will receive title to the property, the rent or lease payments are not deductible on line 20. This is common under conditional sales contracts.

- If part of each rent payment is applied toward an equity interest in the property, you can't deduct on line 20 any of the rent you pay. This is common in lease-purchase options.

- Rent paid in advance is not deductible on line 20. If you pay rent in advance, you can deduct only the amount that applies to your use of the property during the tax year.

- You can't take a deduction for payment of unreasonable rent. This sometimes happens when you rent from a relative. Rent paid to a related person is reasonable if it's about the same amount you would pay to an unrelated third party.

  For example, if the rent is unreasonable, then only the reasonable portion is deductible. The issue of unreasonable rent is a consideration when you and the lessor (the owner of the property) are related. Even if you are related to the owner of the property, the rent may be deductible if it is the amount that you would pay in an arm's length transaction when the owner is not related. The IRS has specific definitions for related persons that are stated in detail in IRS *Publication 538: Accounting Periods and Methods*.

- If you lease a retail space, such as in an antique mall or a station in a hair styling salon, you may pay rent plus a percentage of your sales as a commission. In this case, deduct your lease payments on line 20b. But deduct the commissions you pay on line 10, "Commissions and fees."

- If you rent space for business signs, such as billboards, that rent expense is deducted on line 8, "Advertising."

- If you rent a physical booth or other equipment for trade shows, those expenses are deducted on line 8, "Advertising."

LINE 21

Repairs and Maintenance

Repairs you make to business equipment, office space, buildings and other property are deductible on line 21. Maintenance that you perform is also deductible on line 21.

You must distinguish between repairs and improvements. Repairs and maintenance keep your property in ordinary and efficient operating condition. Those costs are deducted on this line. Improvements add to the value of the property or prolong its useful life. Improvements are considered capital expenditures and must be added to the cost basis of the property. Improvements aren't deducted on line 21. They must be recognized as expense through depreciation, which is reported on line 13.

Also, if you added the expenses of repairs and maintenance to your cost of goods sold, you can't take another deduction for the same expense on line 21.

When figuring the cost of repairs, include supplies and labor. But, you can't deduct the cost or value of your own labor to complete the repairs or maintenance.

If you take the home office deduction, repairs and maintenance performed on your house are not deductible on line 21. Those expenses are reported on Form 8829, Expenses For Business Use of Your Home.

Examples of repairs versus improvements:

- The carpet in your office gets torn. If you simply repair the tear, deduct the expense on line 21. But if you completely replace the carpet in your office, that's an improvement. The cost isn't deductible on line 21.

- Repainting the inside of your office or building is maintenance. Remodeling is an improvement. Repainting the exterior of your building is maintenance. Installing aluminum siding is an improvement.

- Fixing a leak in the roof is a repair. Replacing the roof is an improvement.

- Replacing a computer hard drive that crashed is a repair. Adding memory to a computer is an improvement. Replacing a floppy disk drive that is broken with another floppy drive is a repair. Replacing it with a CD-ROM or DVD drive is an improvement.

- Performing regular maintenance on a copy machine is deductible on line 21. Replacing worn parts in the machine is a repair. Replacing the entire motor is an improvement because it prolongs the life of the machine. Consumables, such as toner, are supplies and deducted on line 22, "Supplies."

- Reupholstering, refinishing or restoring tattered furniture is an improvement.

LINE 22

Supplies

This category includes consumable supplies—items that your business uses and replaces. Many of the items that fall into this category are small and seemingly insignificant. That means many sole proprietors overlook the expenses. That's a mistake. These costs add up fast over the course of year. And every dollar you can deduct on this line will reduce your taxes.

If you work from your home office, but don't take the home office deduction, you can still deduct your expenses for office supplies on line 22.

Examples of supplies to include on line 22

- Toner cartridges for fax machines, printers and copiers
- Pens, paper, notebooks, file folders, paperclips, scissors, rubber bands
- Appointment books and desk calendars
- Wallboards, blackboards and wall calendars
- Receipt and mileage notebooks
- Desk accessories such as pen and paperclip holders
- Light bulbs, thumbtacks, extension cords
- Floppy disks and CD-ROMs

- Business cards, letterhead and envelopes
- Briefcases and cases to carry notebook computers
- Notepads, unless they're imprinted with your business name and used as promotional items, then deduct them as advertising.
- Labels, rubber stamps, staplers and staples

When to deduct the expense of supplies

Generally, you deduct the cost of supplies in the year that you buy and use them. You can also deduct expenses for incidental supplies that are on hand at the end of the tax year if you meet both of these requirements:

- You don't keep records of when supplies are used
- You don't take an inventory of supplies at the beginning and end of the tax year

If your situation fits these parameters, then you can deduct on line 22 the actual amount you spent on these supplies.

Items NOT deductible on line 22

- Computer software. Software is generally capitalized and recognized as expense through depreciation, which is deducted on line 13, "Depreciation and section 179 expense."
- Cleaning supplies. Those are deducted on line 18, "Office expense."
- Supplies that go toward making finished goods. Report the expense of those supplies on line 38, "Materials and supplies," as a part of cost of goods sold.
- Items used to decorate your office. Those expenses are generally deducted on line 18, "Office expense."
- Publications. If you buy business-related magazines, journals and newspapers for use by you or your employees, deduct the cost on line 48, "Other expenses." If you purchase publications for use in a customer waiting room, report the expenses on line 18, "Office expense."
- If you maintain an employee lunchroom or lounge, don't deduct the costs of paper products you buy to stock the room (such as paper cups, plates and utensils) on line 22. Report those expenses on line 18, "Office expense." If you provide snacks or soft drinks, those items are considered employee fringe benefits. Report those costs on line 14, "Employee benefit programs."

- Footrests and chair mats aren't considered supplies. Report those costs on line 18, "Office expense."

- Inexpensive surge protectors are included on line 22. But a longer-lasting, more expensive, uninterruptible power supply (UPS) is considered a piece of equipment. Deduct the cost on line 13, "Depreciation and section 179 expense."

- Telephone answering machine. Report that deduction on line 13.

LINE 23

Taxes and Licenses

You can deduct various business taxes, licenses and permits on line 23. But be careful. Certain taxes and licenses that are considered business expenses are reported on other lines of Schedule C rather than on line 23.

Employment taxes

If you have employees, you withhold the employee's share of Social Security, Medicare, state income and federal income taxes. All of the taxes that you withhold from the paychecks of your employees are already included in employee compensation and are reported on line 26, "Wages," not on line 23.

However, you must also pay the employer's share of Social Security and Medicare taxes, federal unemployment taxes (FUTA), and state unemployment taxes (SUI). The total amount is reported on line 23.

As an employer, you may also be required to make payments to a state unemployment fund or a state disability benefit fund. Deduct those payments as taxes on line 23.

 Caution: Don't deduct your self-employment tax or federal income taxes on line 23.

Business licenses and permits

License and regulatory fees you pay to state or local governments are generally deductible on line 23. These may include sales permits and business licenses.

However, some licenses and fees related to starting your business may have to be amortized. See IRS *Publication 535, Business Expenses*, for more information.

Certain government-granted licenses and permits are not deductible on line 23. These include liquor licenses, taxicab licenses and licenses issued for television or radio broadcasting. If you have a question about the deductibility of a license, see IRS *Publication 535, Business Expenses*, for more information.

Personal property tax

You can deduct taxes imposed by a state or local government on personal property you use in your business. Personal property includes furniture, fixtures and office equipment.

You can also deduct registration fees for the right to use property within a state or local area.

 Caution: If you claim business use of a vehicle, don't deduct license and registration fees or personal property taxes on line 23. If you report actual expenses, those are deducted on line 9, "Car and truck expenses." If you use the standard mileage rate, you can't take an additional deduction for the fees and taxes.

State and local sales taxes

State and local sales taxes that you pay in the course of doing business aren't generally deductible on line 23, but are included as an additional cost of the underlying expense item.

For instance, if you pay for a service, such as the printing of brochures, you may also pay a sales tax that's included in the total cost of the job. That tax is reported as part of the service. It's not separated out and reported on line 23.

If you purchase property (such as a computer) for your business, the sales tax is treated as part of the cost of the property. Don't deduct the sales tax on line 23.

If you buy property or merchandise for resale, the sales tax, if any, is reported as part of the cost of the merchandise. Don't deduct the sales tax on line 23, instead those costs would be part of the costs of the merchandise which would ultimately be included as a costs of goods sold when the property is indeed sold. If the property is depreciable, add the sales tax to the basis of the asset for depreciation.

Some state and local governments impose sales tax on the *seller* of goods or services. If you collect those taxes, and include them in your gross receipts or sales you can deduct them as a business expense on line 23.

 Caution: Some states and local governments impose sales tax on *buyers*. If you collect those taxes from customers and pay those taxes to state or local governments, don't deduct those taxes on line 23. Those taxes are not reported in your gross receipts or sales, so they aren't a deductible business expense.

Real estate taxes

You can deduct on line 23 real estate taxes you pay on buildings, land and other business property.

Generally, you can't deduct taxes that local governments may charge for improvements that increase the value of your property. That includes assessments for improvements such as roads, sewer lines, sidewalks, water mains and public parking facilities.

Also, don't deduct utility expenses on this line. Charges for utilities such as water and sewerage are reported on line 25, "Utilities."

 Caution: If you work from a home office, the real estate taxes you pay on your house aren't deductible on line 23. Report those on Form 8829, Expenses for Business Use of Your Home.

Other expenses deductible on line 23

- Excise taxes
- Occupational taxes charged by a locality
- Federal highway use tax
- State taxes levied on gross income that are directly attributable to your trade or business

Expenses NOT deductible on line 23

- Income taxes. Most income taxes, including federal income taxes, can't be deducted as a business expense. You can generally deduct personal state and local income taxes as an itemized deduction on Schedule A, but those items aren't included on line 23.

- Fuel taxes. Taxes on gasoline, diesel fuel and other motor fuels that you use in your business are included as part of the cost of the fuel. Don't deduct these taxes as a separate item on line 23.

- Estate and gift taxes.

For more information

You can get more information about taxes and licenses in these IRS publications:

- *Publication 535, Business Expenses*
- *Publication 551, Basis of Assets*
- *Publication 378, Fuel Tax Credits and Refunds*
- *Publication 533, Self-Employment Tax*
- *Publication 15, Circular E, Employer's Tax Guide*

LINE 24 (a, b, c and d)

Travel, meals, and entertainment

Line 24 is one of the most frequently used by small-business owners – travel, meals, and entertainment. This line is also one of the most confusing on Schedule C. To help you work through this line, we'll provide step-by-step instructions for each section.

First, be aware that travel expenses are treated differently than meals and entertainment on line 24.

Travel expenses are reported on line 24a. You can deduct 100 percent of travel costs that qualify as business expenses.

Meals and entertainment expenses are reported on line 24b. On line 24b you'll report 100 percent of your costs for meals and entertainment that qualify as business expenses. But, the actual deduction you can take for these expenses is limited. So on lines 24c and 24d you'll calculate your deductible meals and entertainment expenses.

Line 24a Travel

To deduct a travel expense on line 24a, the expense must meet **all** of these requirements:

❑ The expense must be incurred while traveling overnight away from your tax home. Your tax home is your place of business, regardless of where you live. If you qualify for the home office deduction, your tax home and family home are the same.

❑ The expense must be an ordinary and necessary business expense. An ordinary expense is one that is common and accepted in your trade or industry. A necessary expense is one that is helpful and appropriate for your business.

❑ The expense must be reasonable considering your specific business circumstances. You can certainly fly first class. You can stay at the best hotel in town. The IRS gives you some leeway on these expenses, but you can't deduct extravagant or lavish expenses. Use your best business judgment here.

❑ The expense must be incurred for your existing business. You can't deduct travel expenses you incur when starting or acquiring a new business. However, you may be eligible to amortize travel expenses in connection with a business startup. See the discussion of business startup expenses under Part V, "Other expenses," in this book.

Here are some of the common expenses you report on line 24a:

- Lodging
- Air, bus and rail fare
- Tips for lodging, baggage handling, taxi cabs, etc.
- Laundry and dry cleaning
- Local transportation at your destination, including airport shuttle, rental car and taxi fare
- Fax services and Internet connections

 Caution: If you travel overnight using your own car, don't deduct your automobile expenses on line 24a. Instead deduct those costs on line 9, "Car and truck expenses."

 Caution: On line 24a, don't deduct the cost of meals while traveling for business. Meal expenses are deducted on line 24b.

Sooner or later every small-business owner encounters this question: How do I handle travel that combines a business purpose with a personal purpose? The IRS is clear about the answer. You can deduct your travel expenses to and from the destination only if the trip is related primarily to your existing business. This rule holds true even if you conduct some business activities during a trip that is primarily personal.

To determine whether your trip is primarily business or personal, consider the amount of time you spend on activities. If you devote most of your time to business activities, then the trip is considered primarily business. If you spend most of the trip on personal activities, then the trip is obviously personal.

If you take a trip that is primarily personal, and you conduct some business while at your destination, you can deduct those expenses that would otherwise qualify as business expenses.

 Caution: Evaluate your travel expenses on your facts and circumstances. And keep detailed documentation for those trips you deduct.

Here's an example of a primarily personal trip. Harry is an independent sales representative. He sells lighting products to big companies. He and his wife fly from Dallas to Denver to go skiing for a week. While in Denver, Harry takes three days to visit wholesale lighting shops. He spends $70 on taxi fare to visit the shops. Because his trip was primarily personal, Harry can't deduct any airfare or lodging costs as travel expenses. But he can deduct $70 in taxi fares because that cost was directly related to business activities.

As you can see in the above example, the motive and intent for the trip is paramount. On the other hand, if Harry took a business trip to Denver to spend 3 days visiting wholesale lighting shops, the case could be argued that the trip was a business trip. If the skiing was incidental to the business trip, Harry's part of the airfare, meals and lodging could be deductible travel.

Here's another example. Tricia develops database software for small companies. To keep up with the latest technology, she travels to the annual Comdex trade show in Las Vegas, Nevada. She spends each day attending the trade show, seminars and conferences. In the evenings, she visits with her family who lives in Las Vegas. Tricia can deduct all of her travel expenses to Las Vegas because the trip was related **primarily** to her business. However, the fees she pays to attend the trade show, conferences and seminars aren't deducted on line 24a because they're not travel expenses. Instead, she deducts those costs in Part V, "Other expenses," of Schedule C.

Here's a final example. Rick owns a gift shop in New Orleans. Each year he travels to New York City to see the latest retail offerings at the Gift Show Convention. This year, he takes his wife and two children with him to New York. They fly to New York and stay in a hotel suite for three days. Each day, Rick attends the convention. In the evenings, he and his family go to dinner and a play. As travel expenses, Rick can deduct his airfare and lodging (but not that for his family), as well as the transportation costs of getting to and from the hotel and the convention site. All of those expenses are directly related to his business. Rick can't deduct the cost of meals for his family, transportation costs for himself or his family in the evenings or tickets to plays for himself or his family. Those are personal expenses.

You must have adequate records to substantiate all travel deductions. These records must show the amount, time and place, and the business purpose of each expense. Using an expense log is the best way to keep these records. Each day, document your business activities and note any out-of-pocket expenses for which you don't receive a receipt. Always get receipts and keep them with your travel log. The IRS requires that you keep receipts for all lodging expenses (regardless of the amount) and for any expense of more the $75.

Line 24b Meals and Entertainment

On line 24b report **100 percent** of the costs of your business meals and entertainment. This includes meals and entertainment expenses you incur while traveling on business **overnight** as well as meal and entertainment expenses you incur in the city of your business.

Again, these expenses must be ordinary and necessary business expenses. An ordinary expense is one that is common and accepted in your trade or industry. A necessary expense is one that is helpful and appropriate for your business.

Deductible business meals fall into three different categories:

- Meals when you conduct business with business associates or employees while in your city of business
- Meals when you conduct business with business associates while you're traveling overnight on a business trip
- Meals when you dine alone while you're traveling overnight on a business trip

To deduct a meal expense on line 24b, the expense must meet **all** of these requirements:

- ❑ You (or one of your employees) must be present. If one of your employees takes the prospective client to lunch to discuss business, the meal is deductible.
- ❑ The meal is not lavish or extravagant. There are times when nothing less than a four-star restaurant will do. The IRS recognizes this and gives you some latitude. Use your business judgment.
- ❑ The meal is directly related to or associated with the active conduct of your business.

To be directly related, the meal expense must meet these requirements:

- ❑ You realistically expect the meal will specifically benefit your business in some way.
- ❑ During the meal, you engaged in business discussions with clients.

The associated – with test is more lenient. Under this test, if you engage in business discussions either directly before or after the meal, then the meal expense is deductible.

There may be times when you must buy a meal for a business associate and the associate's spouse or employee. This often happens when clients from out-of-town come to your city to conduct business. It might be impractical or impolite to invite the customer to dinner without also extending the invitation to the spouse or employee. In those circumstances, if the meal meets the qualifications for deductibility, the expense is deductible.

Some meal expenses aren't deductible. If you dine alone while conducting local business, the cost of the meal isn't deductible. Meals for your spouse or family members aren't deductible.

Let's look at some examples.

Rob drives from Houston to Chattanooga for a business trip. Once in Chattanooga, he stays for two days. During his time there, he buys lunch for two business associates. Then he drives back to Houston. Rob's meal expenses for the trip – including his time in Chattanooga – total $225. All of his meal expenses are deductible. He dined alone while traveling on a business trip. And he dines with business associates for the purpose of conducting business.

Here's another example. Sarah leaves her home office and drives across town for a meeting with her accountant. After the meeting, Sarah goes alone to a restaurant for lunch. She then returns to her home office. Her meal isn't deductible because she dined alone in the local area of which her home business is located.

Here's a final example. Judy is a fashion designer. Her client, Ted, comes to town to discuss buying some of Judy's designs. Ted visits Judy's show room in the afternoon and purchases some of her designs. Ted's wife has accompanied him on his business trip, and that evening Judy takes Ted and his wife to dinner. The meal expense is deductible for Judy because it is associated with the active conduct of her business. She can deduct the dinner expense for Ted's wife because it would have been impolite to treat an out-of-town client to dinner without inviting the spouse.

You must have documentation to substantiate your meal deductions. This documentation can be in the form of a receipt or be detailed in an expense log. In either case, you must note the business relationship of the people participating in the meal, amount, time and place, and business purpose. If the meal costs more that $75, the IRS requires that you have a receipt.

 Caution: Be sure to report *100 percent* of your meals on line 24b.

Entertainment expenses can include meals as discussed above. But it can also include much more. Entertainment is any activity that provides amusement or recreation. Tickets to sporting events and theatres qualify as entertainment, for example.

To be deductible, entertainment expenses must be ordinary and necessary business expenses. They must be incurred while entertaining an existing customer, a potential client, a business associate or employee.

In addition, entertainment expenses must be either directly related to or associated with the active conduct of your business. (See the preceding explanation under meal expense deductibility.)

Let's look at some examples.

Janis is a dentist. Once a month, she invites various dentists to the theater and to dinner afterward. Janis pays for the tickets and the dinner for all of the dentists. At the dinners, the dentists discuss new procedures and technologies. Janis can deduct the cost of the theater tickets and the dinners as an entertainment expense because it is associated with the active conduct of her business. Janis discussed business after the entertainment event.

Here's another example. Ken writes screenplays. He attends a convention for agents and directors. At the convention, Ken maintains a hospitality suite where he can meet and greet agents and directors. The cost of the hospitality suite is a deductible entertainment expense because it is directly related to his business. Ken realistically expected to find an agent or director to buy his screenplay.

Here's a final example. Mark invites Tom to join him for a round of golf at a club where Mark is a member. During the round, the two men discuss ways they can promote their business together. Mark pays for the round of golf. He also buys drinks and snacks in the clubhouse. He can deduct the golfing costs and the drinks and snacks as expenses on line 24b. However, he can't deduct the dues he pays to be a member of the golf club.

There are restrictions on entertainment expenses. Here are some examples of expenses that are NOT deductible as entertainment:

- Dues for a golf or athletic club, even if you regularly entertain clients or business associates at the club

- Fees paid to a hunting club

- Fees paid for a "dinner" or "supper" club

 Caution: Be sure to report *100 percent* of your entertainment expenses and *100 percent* of your meals expenses on line 24b.

Line 24c

On line 24c, enter 50 percent of the total that you reported on line 24b. This is your nondeductible meals and entertainment expense.

 Caution: For the year 2004, only 50 percent of meal and entertainment expenses were deductible. However, in future years, the IRS may increase the amount of deductions you can take for meals and entertainment. Before completing line 24c, always look in the instructions for Schedule C to find the current year's deduction limit.

Line 24d

Subtract line 24c from line 24b. This is the actual amount of your meals and entertainment deduction.

For more information

Other rules apply for foreign conventions, sky-box rentals and luxury water travel. For more detailed explanations about the expenses covered in this chapter, read IRS *Publication 463, Travel, Entertainment, Gift and Car Expenses.*

Two Other publications might also be helpful:

- *Publication 334, Tax Guide for Small Business*
- *Publication 535, Business Expenses*

LINE 25

Utilities

The costs of utilities for your business are deductible on line 25. These include:

- Electricity
- Gas, propane and heating oil
- Water
- Sewerage
- Landfill charges for trash and refuse

Expenses NOT deductible on line 25

- Utilities for your home, even if you claim the home office deduction. Instead, deduct the portion of utilities used for your home office on Form 8829, line 19.
- Utilities paid for some other person or business. Unless the utilities are used in your trade or business, they are a non-deductible personal expense.
- Utilities in your home for business purposes, but for which you have not claimed (or do not qualify for) the home office deduction.

LINE 26

Wages

Report on line 26 wages you pay your employees. This includes salaries, commissions, bonuses and other compensation.

However, if you're a manufacturer, not all of your employees' wages will be deducted on line 26. The wages you pay production workers, supervisors and indirect factory workers are deducted on line 37 under cost of goods sold in Part III.

For example, you manufacture key chains. You have two production workers who make the key chains. You also have an administrative assistant who handles office duties. In this case, the wages for your two production workers are reported on line 37 as part of your cost of goods. The wages for your administrative assistant are reported on line 26.

Business owner's income

Although you can deduct wages you pay to employees on line 26, you can't deduct money that you pay yourself. The net earnings from self-employment are represented by the "bottom line" of your Schedule C, regardless of how much money you actually pay yourself during the year. Therefore, don't include payments to yourself on line 26 or on any other line of Schedule C.

Reimbursed employee expenses

For tax purposes, reimbursed employee expenses can be treated in two different ways, depending upon whether the reimbursements are made under an "accountable plan" or a "nonaccountable plan." As you'll see, an accountable plan requires more record keeping, but it will save you and your employees money.

- Accountable plan

    Under an accountable plan, reimbursements are excluded from the employee's gross income. You don't include the reimbursements in an employee's wages, so you don't deduct the reimbursements on line 26. Instead, deduct the reimbursed expenses in the categories to which they pertain. For instance, if you reimburse an employee for travel, you deduct that expense on line 24a, "Travel, meals and entertainment."

So what qualifies as an accountable plan? You have an accountable plan if you meet three requirements:

❏ The reimbursements are deductible business expenses the employee incurs while working for you.

❏ You require substantiation for the expenses. Employees must provide a log, account book, statement of expense or similar record that details the expense. Details to support the expense include amount, time, use and business purpose, as well as receipts to document expenses.

❏ Employees must provide substantiation of expenses within about 60 days and return any excess reimbursements to you within about 120 days.

- Unaccountable plan

  Reimbursements made under an unaccountable plan are included in an employee's wages. You report them on IRS Form W-2. Deduct all W-2 wages on line 26.

  Because you treat reimbursements as part of employee's compensation, you're required to withhold income and employment taxes on the reimbursements. You also have to pay the employer's portion of payroll taxes on the reimbursed amounts.

Employment credits

If you hire workers who meet certain employment requirements, you may be entitled to tax credits. These credits are then deducted from your total cost of wages reported on line 26. You must complete the following forms before claiming an employment credit:

- Form 5884, Work Opportunity Credit
- Form 8844, Empowerment Zone Employment Credit
- Form 8845, Indian Employment Credit
- Form 8861, Welfare-to-Work Credit

Expenses NOT deductible on line 26

- Employee fringe benefits. Deduct expenses for fringe benefits on line 14, "Employee benefit programs."
- Pension, profit-sharing and retirement plans. Report those expenses on line 19, "Pension and profit-sharing plans."

- Wages that you report on line 37 under cost of goods sold.
- Commissions and fees you pay to independent contractors. Report those expenses on line 10, "Commissions and fees."

For more information

See these IRS publications for more help:
- *Publication 15, Circular E, Employer's Tax Guide*
- *Publication 15-A, Employer's Supplemental Tax Guide*
- *Publication 15-B, Employer's Tax Guide to Fringe Benefits*
- *Publication 535, Business Expenses*

LINE 27

Other Expenses

Include on this line any expenses that you haven't categorized on other lines within Schedule C.

However, an important part of the preparation of your Schedule C is the appropriate classification of expenses. It's easy to allow yourself to include items as other expense that should be classified elsewhere.

The IRS also recognizes this, since each item that you include on line 27 as an other expense must also be detailed on line 48, of Part V of Schedule C. In fact the detail listed in Part V and summarized on line 48 is the amount to be included on line 27, so the two are really the same information.

Therefore, for a detailed discussion of expenses to include on line 27, See Part V, Line 48 in this book for more information.

Again, the key point is not to include items here just because it is easy. Take the time to evaluate the most appropriate line for each business expense. Only include amounts on line 48 and line 27 that do not fit on any other lines of Schedule C.

LINE 28

Total Expenses

This line tallies up all of your business expenses except business use of your home. Add lines 8 through 27 and enter the total on line 28, "Total expenses."

Tips

- Don't include expenses for the business use of your home on line 28.

- Don't forget to carry over your total other expenses from Schedule C, page 2, Part V, line 48, to page 1, Part II, line 27.

- Make sure that you've reported each expense in its proper category. Also make sure that you haven't reported an expense more than once. For instance, if you hire an outplacement firm to help secure new jobs for laid-off employees, that expense is reported on line 17, "Legal and professional services." Make sure you don't also include that expense in Part V "Other Expenses" on line 48.

- Check your addition of lines 8 through 27.

- Finally, check your addition again.

LINE 29

Tentative Profit (or Loss)

Subtract line 28 from line 7 in Part I. This is your tentative profit or loss. It doesn't include the deductible expenses for the business use of your home. We'll get to that next.

If you have a loss, enter the figure in parentheses (xxx) on line 29.

If you show a profit, congratulations. Keep up the good work.

Tip

Check your math at least twice. Mathematical discrepancies are the number one reason that the IRS changes the tax information submitted via tax returns. So check your math now to save yourself a few headaches later.

LINE 30

Expenses For Business Use Of Your Home (Including Form 8829)

The expenses associated with maintaining a home office are deductible on line 30. But before you can claim a deduction, you must complete Form 8829, Expenses for Business Use of Your Home.

Later in this section, we'll go through Form 8829 line-by-line. First, however, you must determine whether or not your home office qualifies for the deduction.

Regular and exclusive use

To claim a deduction on Schedule C for the use of your home office, the office space must be used "regularly" *and* "exclusively" for business.

Meeting the exclusivity test is usually the most for difficult small-business owners. Exclusive means that the space is used solely for business. If your office has a TV that your kids use to play video games, the space is not used exclusively for business. If you use the space to entertain guests or house your mother-in-law when she visits, the space is not used exclusively for business. If your office doesn't meet the exclusivity test, then you can't take the home office deduction.

There are some exceptions to the exclusive rule.

The first exception is storage. You can deduct expenses for space that you use for business storage if your home office is the only office location for your business. You can take the deduction even if you store business and personal items in the same area.

The second exception to exclusivity is if your business is a day-care center operated from your home. In this case the space can be used for a day-care facility and for personal purposes. You must allocate the amount of time you use the space for day care and the amount of time that you use the space for your family. We'll talk more about this usage later.

Your home office space must also meet **one** of these qualifications:

- It is your principle or main place of business.
- It is a place where your customers meet with you in the normal course of your business.
- It is a separate structure, not attached to your home that is used exclusively in your trade or business.

Form 8829
Expenses for the Business Use of Your Home

If you meet the requirements outlined earlier, then you must complete Form 8829 to take the home office deduction.

Complete a separate Form 8829 for each home that you used for business during the year. These line-by-line instructions will help you correctly complete Form 8829.

Name of proprietor

Enter the name of the business owner on this line. Don't enter your business name. Also enter the business owner's Social Security number. Don't enter your Employer Identification number (EIN).

Part I

Part of Your Home Used For Business

LINE 1 (Form 8829)

Enter the area in square feet of your home that you use exclusively for business. Include space you use for business storage.

Use square footage to calculate your home office area. If you use one room for your home office, and the room is 12 feet by 15 feet, then your home office area is 180 square feet (length multiplied by width). If you use more than one room exclusively for your business, calculate the total square footage for all rooms and enter it on line 1.

If you operate a day-care facility, enter the total square footage you use, even if the space is used for business and personal purposes.

LINE 2 (Form 8829)

Enter the total square footage of your home, including the area used for a home office or a day-care facility.

LINE 3 (Form 8829)

Divide line 1 by line 2. This is the percentage of the space used as your home office compared to the total area of your home.

For example, your home is 2,000 square feet. Your home office area is 180 square feet. The figure you enter is .09, (180 divided by 2,000).

LINES 4 through 6 (Form 8829)

If your business is not a day-care center, skip these lines and go to line 7. If you operate a day-care facility in your home, complete lines 4 through 6.

Lines 4 through 6 adjust the overall percentage on line 3 for day-care centers that do not use the space exclusively for business.

On line 4, enter the total number of hours that you used the space as a day-care center during the year. To make the calculation, multiply the total number days you used the space as a day-care center by the number of hours per day that you used it.

For example, you used the space eight hours per day for 200 days during year. Multiply 8 by 200. Your total is 1,600 hours. Enter 1,600 on line 4.

Line 5 is already completed for you. Don't enter anything on this line.

Divide line 4 by line 5. Enter the result on line 6. This is the percentage of the total hours available that you used the space for the day care. In our example, the percentage would be 18 (1,600 divided by 8,784), therefore, enter .18 on line 6.

LINE 7 (Form 8829)

This line reports the percentage of business use of your home. If you don't operate a day-care facility in your home, simply enter on line 7 the percentage you reported on line 3.

If you operate a day-care center, multiply line 6 by line 3 and enter the total on line 7.

Line 7 is now the percentage of your home that is used for business. This is a key figure in your tax calculations and will impact the amount of expenses you can claim for your home office deduction.

 Caution: Check your math before moving on to the remainder of Form 8829.

Part II
Figure Your Allowable Deduction

LINE 8 (Form 8829)

On line 8 enter the total net earnings from your business, before the inclusion of the expenses related to the home office. This amount can be found on your Schedule C line 29, "Tentative profit (loss)."

Also include on line 8 any gains related to your home that you reported on Form 1040, Schedule D. You may have such gains or losses if you sold your home during the year.

If you have an office in addition to your home office, then you'll need to allocate the earnings from the business between the offices. If this applies to you, see the instructions for Form 8829 for additional detail.

The home office deduction is limited to the earnings from your business. So if you don't have earnings from your business, a portion of the home office deduction as calculated on Form 8829 will not be deductible. However, even if you show a loss on line 8, you may still be entitled to deductions found later on Form 8829.

Direct and indirect expenses on lines 9 through 21

The amounts to be reported on lines 9 through 21 are the actual expenses you paid during the year to maintain your home and your home office. These expenses must be classified as either "direct" or "indirect." The distinction is important because *all* direct expenses are deductible, but only a *portion* of indirect expenses is deductible.

- Direct Expenses: These are expenses that are specific to your home office and are not related to any other part of the house. These expenses only benefit the business portion of the house. Direct expenses could include utilities if your home office has separate utility meters. Painting or repairs made only to the home office space are direct expenses. Report your direct expenses in column (a). Don't include any direct expenses in column (b).

- Indirect Expenses: These are expenses that benefit the entire house, including the space used for your home office. Utilities supplied to the entire house, mortgage interest related to the home loan and real estate taxes levied on the entire property are examples of indirect expenses. Report indirect expenses in column (b). Don't include any indirect expenses in column (a).

Lines 9 through 11

The expenses you report on lines 9 through 11 include casualty losses (line 9), mortgage interest (line 10) and real estate taxes (line 11). Enter only amounts on these lines that would be deductible whether or not you used part of your home for a business. For instance, if your mortgage interest deduction is limited on Form 1040, Schedule A, enter on line 10 only the portion that is deductible on your Schedule A.

Even if you reported a loss on line 8, these amounts may be deductible as a business expense in future years. They will, in effect, increase your loss from the business in the current year. This loss will be available to offset business income in future years.

LINE 9 (Form 8829)

On line 9, enter casualty losses that you incurred during the year. Don't forget to differentiate between direct casualty losses and indirect casualty losses.

If you had a qualifying casualty loss during the year, you must complete IRS Form 4684, Casualties and Thefts. On line 9 report the amount from Form 4684, line 18.

On Form 4684, the amount of casualty losses that you may qualify for can be limited based on your adjusted gross income. The amount from Form 4684, line 18, that you include on Form 8829, line 9, is only the amount that would have been allowed if you deducted the amount on Form 1040, Schedule A. The remainder, the excess casualty losses, will be reported on line 27 of Form 8829.

LINE 10 (Form 8829)

Enter deductible mortgage interest that you paid on the house where your home office is located. Don't include mortgage interest on properties such as second homes. Include on line 10 only the amount of mortgage interest you can deduct on Form 1040, Schedule A. If you have excess mortgage interest, that amount will be deducted later on Form 8829.

LINE 11 (Form 8829)

Enter real estate taxes you paid on the house where your home office is located.

Don't include real estate taxes you paid on other properties, such as a second home.

LINE 12 (Form 8829)

Add lines 9 through 11 column (a). Enter the total on line 12 (a).

Add lines 9 through 11 column (b). Enter the total on line 12 (b).

These are the total direct and indirect expenses of maintaining your home.

LINE 13 (Form 8829)

Multiply the total on line 12 (b) by the percentage from line 7. Enter the result on line 13.

Line 13 determines the percentage of indirect costs that are deductible, based on the percentage of square footage your home office occupies in your house.

Most small-business owners who take the home office deduction don't have direct costs to report on lines 9 through 11. Since most use a room within their houses as the home office, they don't have a separate mortgage or a separate real estate tax bill related to a specific room. So don't be confused if column (a) for lines 9 through 11 is blank on your Form 8829.

LINE 14 (Form 8829)

Add the total from line 12 column (a) and line 13. Enter the result on line 14.

 Caution: Be careful on this one. Be sure to use the total on line 12(a) and the total on line 13. *Do not use the total that is included on line 12(b).*

LINE 15 (Form 8829)

Subtract line 14 from line 8. Enter the total on line 15. If the answer is zero or less, enter 0.

Lines 16 through 21

These lines are similar to lines 9 through 11. On each of these lines, continue to differentiate between direct and indirect expenses, as discussed above. It's possible that you won't have any expenses to report in column (a) since those apply specifically to your home office, not to your entire home.

LINE 16 (Form 8829)

Enter excess mortgage interest you paid related to your home. This is the amount that would not be deductible on Schedule A.

LINE 17 (Form 8829)

Enter the amount of insurance that you paid related to your home. This includes property insurance as well as liability insurance.

LINE 18 (Form 8829)

Enter the total amount you paid for repair and maintenance on your home.

Be sure to differentiate between direct and indirect expenses on this line. If a repair is related solely to the home office, make sure you include the amount in column (a), direct expenses.

 Caution: The expenses of improvements made to your home aren't deductible on this line. Only the costs of repairs are deductible. Improvements increase the value or extend the life of your home. Repairs keep your house in good working condition. For example, replacing a few roof shingles is a repair. Replacing the whole roof is an improvement.

LINE 19 (Form 8829)

Enter the total utilities paid in connection with your home. Include payments for electricity, gas, water, sewer, security, etc. Don't enter any telephone expenses on this line.

LINE 20 (Form 8829)

Enter all other expenses related to the maintenance and operation of your home. This is the catch all line for expenses not listed on other lines.

If you rent rather own your home, include your rental expense on this line.

LINE 21 (Form 8829)

Add lines 16 through 20 column (a). Report the total on line 21 column (a).

Add lines 16 through 20, column (b). Report the total on line 21 column (b).

Make sure you have separated the direct from the indirect expenses.

This line is the total of expenses related to your home office that would not be deductible on your Form 1040, Schedule A.

LINE 22 (Form 8829)

Multiply the total on line 21 column (b) by the percentage on line 7. Enter the result on line 22.

This line reduces the indirect expenses included in lines 16 through 20 to include only the business percentage of those expenses.

LINE 23 (Form 8829)

Enter any unused home office expenses carried over from the previous year. If you have a carry over amount, it will be included on your tax return from last year, on Form 8829, line 41.

LINE 24 (Form 8829)

Add line 21 column (a), line 22 column (b) and line 23 column (b). Enter the total on line 24.

LINE 25 (Form 8829)

Enter the *smaller* of line 15 or line 24.

This line represents your allowable operating expenses.

LINE 26 (Form 8829)

Subtract line 25 from line 15. Enter the result on line 26.

LINE 27 (Form 8829)

On this line, report any excess casualty losses that you did not report on line 9 above.

Here's how to determine the amount of excess casualty loss:

- If you had a casualty loss in the current year, you reported it on Form 4684, Casualties and Thefts.
- On line 9 above, you reported the amount of casualty loss that would have been allowed if deducted on Form 1040, Schedule A.
- Subtract line 9 from the total amount you entered on Form 4684, line 18.
- Enter the result on line 27.

LINE 28 (Form 8829)

Before you can report an amount on this line, you must complete Part III, Depreciation of Your Home.

After completing Part III, carry the amount on line 40 to line 28.

LINE 29 (Form 8829)

Include on line 29 any carry over amounts from the prior year for excess casualty losses and depreciation.

Carry over amounts to be included on line 29 of this year's tax return will be on Form 8829, line 42, on your last year's tax return.

LINE 30 (Form 8829)

Add lines 27, 28 and 29. Enter the total on line 30.

This amount represents the total expense for excess casualty losses, depreciation and any carry over amounts from the prior year.

LINE 31 (Form 8829)

Enter the *smaller* of line 26 or line 30.

This is your allowable deduction for excess casualty losses, depreciation and carry over amounts from the prior year.

LINE 32 (Form 8829)

Add lines 14, 25, and 31. Enter the result on line 32.

This line represents the total deductible costs associated with your home office.

LINE 33 (Form 8829)

The casualty losses that are allowed in connection with your home office are deductible, but not on Form 8829.

Enter on line 33 any amounts from line 14 and 31 that relate to casualty losses. Also enter the total from line 33 on Form 4684, Section B.

LINE 34 (Form 8829)

Subtract line 33 from line 32. Enter the result on line 34.

This is your home office deduction. Enter the amount from this line on Schedule C, line 30.

Part III
Depreciation of Your Home

In claiming the home office deduction, you've reclassified a portion of your principle residence as business property. Because this portion is business property, you're allowed a deduction for the use of the asset through depreciation.

The allowed depreciation related to your home office is dependent upon the cost basis that you have in the property, the business percentage related to your home office and IRS prescribed depreciation percentages.

Part III of this form gives you step-by-step instructions on calculating the depreciation related to your home. Keep in mind that you can only deduct depreciation on your home if you claim the home office deduction.

LINE 35 (Form 8829)

Enter the *smaller* of your home's fair market value or its adjusted cost basis.

The fair market value is the amount that you could sell the house for today, including the land or lot on which it sits.

The adjusted cost basis typically includes the price you paid for the house (and land) plus any major improvements you've made.

LINE 36 (Form 8829)

Enter the value of the land that you included on line 35.

For instance, on line 35 you entered $200,000 as the adjusted cost basis of your home. That included the house, valued at $150,000, and the land on which it sits, valued at $50,000.

In that instance, you would enter $50,000 on line 36.

LINE 37 (Form 8829)

Subtract line 36 from line 35. Enter the result on line 37.

The amount on line 37 is now the basis of your home, excluding the land. This is the gross amount that may be depreciated.

LINE 38 (Form 8829)

Multiply line 37 by the percentage on line 7. Enter the result on line 38.

This is the total basis of your home office.

LINE 39 (Form 8829)

On line 39, enter your depreciation percentage.

The percentage to use on line 39 depends upon your specific circumstances.

If you used your home office for the entire year then the percentage to use on line 39 is generally 2.564 percent.

However, if the current year is the first year that you are claiming depreciation for business use of your home, then you will enter a different percentage. To determine the percentage to use, follow these steps:

- Identify the first month you used the home office for business in the chart below
- Report the corresponding percentage on line 39

For example, if you began using your home office in June, enter 1.391 on line 39.

If you first used the home office in	Use the following percentage on line 39
January	2.461%
February	2.247%
March	2.033%
April	1.819%
May	1.605%
June	1.391%
July	1.177%
August	0.963%
September	0.749%
October	0.535%
November	0.321%
December	0.107%

These amounts are based on a straight-line depreciation using a 39-year useful life and then allocated based on how many months you used the property for business. You can find this same chart in the instructions for Form 8829.

LINE 40 (Form 8829)

Multiply line 38 by line 39. Enter the result on line 40. Also report this amount on line 28 of Form 8829.

This is the allowable depreciation related to your home office.

Part IV
Carryover of Unallowed Expenses

LINE 41 (Form 8829)

Subtract line 25 from line 24. Enter the result on line 41. If the amount is than zero, enter 0.

This line represents the total operating expenses associated with your home office that you could not deduct this year. You can carry over this amount to your next year's return.

Tip

It is important for sole proprietors to keep their tax records for at least three years.

LINE 42 (Form 8829)

Subtract line 31 from line 30. Enter the result on line 42. If the amount is less than zero, enter 0.

This line represents the total excess casualty losses and depreciation associated with your home office that you could not deduct this year. You can carry over this amount to your next year's tax return.

Summary

There you have it, the home office deduction, line-by-line. Attach Form 8829 to your Schedule C.

Make sure that you keep all of your calculations and your notes with a copy of your tax return. Those items will not only help substantiate your deduction if necessary, but will also provide you with a roadmap for next year.

For more information

For more help with the home office deduction, read IRS *Publication 587, Business Use of Your Home.*

LINE 31

Net Profit or Loss

This is the final tally, and we are almost there. Subtract line 30 from line 29. Check your math. Once you have checked all of your math take a few minutes and check the math again.

If you show a profit

Congratulations! Your business is in the black. This is your net profit, also called your earned income from self-employment.

The next step is to carry your profit (earned income) amount to Form 1040. Simply take the amount shown on line 31 and enter it on Form 1040, line 12.

Also enter your profit amount on Schedule SE, Self-Employment Tax, line 2.

That's it. Gather up the forms and explanation statements you filled out in conjunction with Schedule C. Attach Schedule C and your supporting forms (SBE for Auto Deductions, 4562 for Depreciation, 8829 for Home Office Deduction, and other supporting statements) to Form 1040.

If you show a loss

If you show a loss, the amount you can deduct in the current year may be limited. Before you enter your loss on line 31, go to line 32. See the next instructions for information about completing line 32 and the amount of the loss that is deductible.

LINE 32

Investment Risk

If you show a loss on line 31, you must check box 32a or 32b to describe your investment in your business activity. If you show a profit on line 31, don't complete line 32.

The loss that you incur from your Schedule C business is limited to the amount that you have "at risk" in the business. This means that the IRS will not allow a deduction for a loss that's greater than the amount of money that you've actually put into the business. The amount "at risk" is more than just your cash. It also includes loans, property, cash and other investments you've made in your business.

Box 32a

Check box 32a if all of your investment in the business is at risk. Your investment is considered "at risk" for the following items:

- Money and property you contribute to the business
- Amounts you borrow for use in the business if you're personally liable for repayment or if you pledge property (other than property used in the business) as security for a loan

If you check box 32a, then carry over the amount of the loss you reported on line 31 to Form 1040, line 12.

 Caution: If you check box 32a, but answered "No" to question G in Part I, you may need to complete Form 8582 to calculate your deductible loss.

Box 32b

Check box 32b if some of your business investment is not at risk. This could include the following:

- Non-recourse loans that are not secured by your own property (other than property used in the business). These loans may have been used to acquire the business, finance the business or to acquire property used in the business. Non-recourse loans are those that you are not personally required to pay back if your business defaults on the loan.
- Cash, property or borrowed amounts used in the business (or contributed to the business or used to acquire the business) that are protected against loss by a guarantee, stop-loss agreement, or other similar arrangement (excluding casualty insurance and insurance against tort liability).
- Amounts borrowed for use in the business from a person who has an interest in the business, other than as a creditor, or who is related to a person (other than you) having such an interest.

Here's the key point to line 32b: If you don't stand to lose the money, then the losses will not be deductible. Generally, if you have amounts in the business for which you are not at risk, you'll have to complete Form 6198 to figure your allowable loss. In addition, if you answered "No" to question G in Part I, your loss may be limited further. See instructions for Form 8582 for details.

For more information

See these IRS publications for more information about at-risk rules:

- *Publication 535, Business Expenses*
- *Publication 925, Passive Activity and At-Risk rules*

PART III:
COST OF GOODS SOLD

If you sell merchandise to produce income for your business, use this section to calculate your cost of goods sold.

This section applies to any business that sells merchandise to customers. If you make or manufacture products, you must complete this section. If you buy merchandise and resell it to customers, you must complete this section—even if you don't keep any inventory on hand.

If you sell merchandise to customers, but have no inventory on hand at the end of the year, you must still complete this section to calculate your cost of goods sold.

If your business doesn't produce merchandise for sale or doesn't buy and resell merchandise, then you don't need to complete this section.

LINE 33

Method used to value closing inventory

Check the box that shows the method you use to determine the value of your closing inventory.

Most sole proprietors use the cost method of inventory valuation. The cost method means that the value of the inventory in your possession is "exactly what you paid for it."

For example, you paid $10 each for 600 toy cars. That $10 includes all costs related to the cars, such as taxes, freight and storage. Your closing inventory is the number of cars you have in your inventory, multiplied by the $10 you paid for each one. Even if market price for the cars have fallen below $10, and you won't be able to sell the cars for more than $7, you still report the full amount you paid for the cars.

If you value your inventories by any method other than cost, check box b or c. Your method of valuing inventory can be any method approved by the IRS.

 Caution: You are **required** to use the cost method of valuing inventory if you use the cash method of accounting.

LINE 34

Was there any change in determining quantities, costs or valuations?

Answer this question yes or no based on your facts and circumstances.

You must answer yes to this question if any of the following apply for the current tax year:

❏ You changed the method by which you value your inventory.

❏ You changed the method by which you account for the amount of items in your inventory.

❏ You changed your inventory accounting methods.

If you answer yes on line 34, you must attach a statement to your Schedule C. In the statement, explain what change you made and how it affected the amount of your closing inventory.

LINE 35

Inventory at beginning of year

The ending inventory for the prior year is the beginning inventory for the current year. You can find this amount on your prior year Schedule C, line 41.

If there's a difference between the opening inventory of the current year and the amount on last year's tax return, attach a schedule to explain the differences. The amounts should match from year to year.

LINE 36

Purchases less cost of items withdrawn for personal use

Simply add up the amounts you paid for merchandise during the year and report the total on this line.

The cost of merchandise that you withdrew from sales must not be included on this line. For example, if you used products for advertising or promotion purposes, the costs of those products are not included on line 36. The cost of merchandise you took for personal use is also excluded on this line.

LINE 37

Cost of labor

Include on this line only the direct and indirect costs of labor to actually produce the merchandise you sell to customers. This line is most frequently completed by businesses in the manufacturing, construction and mining industries.

Let's take an example. You sell appliances. You hire a person to load, unload and stock appliances in your store. Don't report that person's wages on line 37. Instead report that expense on line 26, "Wages."

Here's another example. You make furniture. You hire a man to help you assemble the furniture. You hire a woman to work as a bookkeeper. The man's labor helps you produce your merchandise. The cost of his wages is reported on line 37. But the woman's wages are not deductible on line 37, because she doesn't produce merchandise. Deduct her wages on line 26.

LINE 38

Materials and supplies

Only manufacturers must complete this line.

Report on line 38 only the cost of materials and supplies you use in your manufacturing process.

 Caution: Don't report on line 38 other materials and supplies you use in your business. For instance, office supplies such as pens and paper are reported on line 22, "Supplies."

LINE 39

Other costs

Again, only manufacturers need to complete this line.

Examples of other costs that are included on line 39 include containers, freight-in, and direct or indirect overhead expenses that are necessary expenses of the manufacturing operation.

LINE 40

Add lines 35 through 39

Add your amounts on lines 35 through 39. As always check your addition again and again. An incorrect number here will distort your cost of goods and your net income – and will result in the wrong amount of tax on your tax return.

LINE 41

Inventory at end of year

By now, you've physically counted the items in your inventory on the last day of the year. The inventory list has been "extended" (your cost per item multiplied by the number of items) so that you now have the value of your closing inventory. Report that amount on this line.

Your ending inventory this year will generally be your beginning inventory next year.

LINE 42

Cost of goods sold

This is another "do the math" line item. Subtract line 41 from line 40. Report the total on this line.

This amount represents your cost of the merchandise sold during the tax year. Transfer this amount to Part I, line 4 on page 1 of Schedule C.

PART IV: INFORMATION ON YOUR VEHICLE

There's no business deduction calculated in this in this section. It's an informational section only. But it's critically important. The IRS uses the information in this section to review and substantiate your vehicle deductions on line 9 of Schedule C.

If you're filing Form 4562, Depreciation and Amortization, to depreciate a vehicle used in your business, you don't need to complete this part of Schedule C. Just leave it blank.

If you take a deduction for the business use of a vehicle and don't claim depreciation on the vehicle using Form 4562, then complete the information requested in Part IV.

If you're not claiming car or truck expenses on line 9 of Schedule C, you don't have to complete this section. Just leave it blank.

If you use a fleet of two or more vehicles simultaneously in your business, don't complete Part IV. See line 9 instructions in this book for more information.

Use of more than one vehicle

If you use more than one vehicle in your business during the year (other than a fleet), leave Part IV blank and attach a separate schedule that you create.

For example, you drove one car from January 1 until May 15. You then sold that car and purchased a new one. You drove the new car for the remainder of the year. Or, perhaps your family owns two cars, and you drove both at different times for business purposes.

In those circumstances, you don't complete Part IV. Instead, use a separate sheet of paper to list the information for each of the vehicles you drove. Include on the sheet the exact information for each vehicle that is required in Part IV. On line 43 of Part IV, write "See Attached Schedule." Leave Part IV blank and attach the vehicle schedule you created to page 2 of Schedule C.

LINE 43

When did you place your vehicle in service?

Simply fill in the month, day and year you began using this vehicle in your business. This is considered the "placed in service date."

 Caution: Be sure you use the date that you ***began using the vehicle in your business.*** This date may be different than the date you actually purchased the vehicle.

LINE 44

Total miles you drove

Enter the total number of miles you drove for each individual purpose.

- Line A *Business*: This is for business miles only. Record the total miles you drove this vehicle for business purposes during the year.

- Line B *Commuting*: Enter the miles you used your vehicle for commuting to and from your primary business office. If you claim the home office deduction, you should not report any commuting miles.

- Line C *Other*: In this space enter all miles you drove other than for business and commuting. Include all of the personal miles you drove.

When the miles entered in *Business*, *Commuting* and *Other* are totaled, you'll have recorded all of the miles put on your business vehicle for the year.

LINE 45

Do you have another vehicle for personal use?

If you have a another vehicle other than the one for which you entered miles on line 44, answer this question yes.

If you don't have a vehicle other than the one you use for business, answer the question no.

LINE 46

Was your vehicle available for personal use?

If you were able to use the vehicle for personal purposes at times other than your normal work hours, answer yes to this question.

If not, answer the question no.

 Caution: If you claim the home office deduction, the answer to this question will always be yes.

LINE 47a

Do you have evidence to support your deduction?

The IRS wants to know in advance if you have documents to support the deduction you have taken for the business use of your vehicle.

Certainly, if you take a vehicle expense deduction, you answer this question yes.

If you answer no to the question, then you should not take the vehicle expense deduction. You can't take a deduction based on an estimated amount of miles or expense.

LINE 47b

Is the evidence written?

Answer either yes or no to this question. If you answer yes, be sure that you actually have written documentation that supports your vehicle deduction.

The best evidence to support a vehicle deduction is contemporaneous and written. You should use a log to record the total miles you drive each day. It should show the miles allocated to business, personal, commuting and other (such as medical). For business miles driven, your record should show the purpose of the miles, including names and addresses of places and people visited.

In addition, keep a record of the actual expenses incurred on the vehicle and the receipts. Remember, you can calculate your vehicle deduction using either of two methods: actual expense method or the mileage method. You can use whichever method provides you with the largest deduction. So thorough, contemporaneous, written records concerning your vehicle are valuable resources.

 Caution: You can switch between using the standard mileage method and actual expenses from year to year to get the maximum deduction—but only if you use the mileage method the first year you place the vehicle in service for your business. If you use the actual expense method the first year, you must use that method for the entire time you use that vehicle for business purposes.

PART V: OTHER EXPENSES

In Part V, report business expenses that you didn't report on lines 8 through 26 or on line 30 of Schedule C. Don't take the easy way out and include expenses here that should be included on a separate line of Schedule C.

When reporting expenses on this line, be as specific as possible. List the type and amount of each expense separately in the space provided. If you need to, attach another sheet of paper that provides a line-by-line detail of the total expenses you report on line 48.

The amounts included in Part V are totaled on line 48. You then carry that total forward to line 27 of Schedule C.

Following are some of the common expenses you can report in Part V.

Business banking fees

In Part V, deduct fees you pay in conjunction with business bank accounts. This includes checking, savings and money market accounts. You might incur fees for:

- Service charges
- ATM use
- Overdrafts
- Online bill payments
- Copies of cleared checks
- Duplicate statements
- Debit card use
- Stop payments

Business credit card fees

If you have credit cards that you use exclusively for business, you can deduct the related fees. These might include:

- Annual fees
- Late payment fees
- Fees for going over your line of credit
- Fees for additional or replacement cards
- Cash advance fees

 Caution: In Part V, don't deduct the interest you pay for carrying a balance on your business credit card. Report the interest expense on line 16b, "Other interest."

Business organization dues

Fees and dues to certain business-related organizations are deductible on line 48. These include:

- Chambers of commerce
- Trade associations
- Professional organizations such as bar associations and medical associations
- Civic or public service organizations
- Business leagues
- Boards of trade
- Real estate boards

 Caution: Fees for hotel and airline clubs, country clubs, athletic clubs and the like are not deductible and are therefore not included in Part V. However, if you pay athletic or gym club memberships for your employees, the membership fees are deductible on line 14, "Employee benefit programs."

Telephone, including lines you use for Internet connections

Part of the telephone expenses for your home office may be deductible, even if you don't claim the home office deduction.

The IRS assumes that you have at least one personal telephone line in your home. If you use that one line for business and personal purposes, you can't deduct any of the base-rate or regular fees as a business expense in Part V.

However, if you use that personal line to make long-distance calls related to your business, then the long-distance charges are 100-percent deductible in Part V. When you receive your telephone bill, simply circle the business-related calls, total them up at the end of the year and report that total in Part V.

If you have two or more telephone lines in your home that are used for business purposes, the entire charges for all the lines after the first are deductible, including the base rate. Remember, the lines must be used for business purposes in connection with your active trade or business.

Other common expenses that you can deduct in Part V

- Postage, shipping and delivery fees, except those included as part of cost of goods sold
- State unemployment insurance
- Merchant fees, the amounts credit card companies charge for processing transactions
- Penalties and fines you pay for nonperformance or late performance of a contract
- Small tools, such as screwdrivers and hammers
- Publications and subscriptions to magazines, newsletters and newspapers used in your business
- Gifts that are business-related. These might include gifts to suppliers, clients, contractors and business associates. Gift expenses are limited to $25 per year per recipient. But if you give gifts to employees as part of an achievement award or as a fringe benefit, report that expense on line 14, "Employee benefit programs."
- Anti-virus computer software. In most cases, you must depreciate the cost of computer software. Anti-virus software is the exception. Deduct the full cost in the year you purchase it.
- Part of the cost of qualified clean-fuel vehicles used in your business. Examples of clean fuels include natural gas and hydrogen.
- At-risk loss deduction. If you had a nondeductible loss in the previous year because of at-risk rules, you may be able to deduct that loss on the current year's Schedule C.

Amortizing business startup costs

Startup expenses occur before the day your business opens its doors. Those startup costs can't be deducted as regular business expenses on lines 8 through 26 on Schedule C. Instead certain business startup costs can be amortized and deducted in Part V. By amortizing these costs, you take the deductions over a number of years instead of taking them all at once in the year you start your business.

If your startup expenses actually result in you launching a business, you can amortize the costs in Part V. That means you deduct the startup expenses in equal installments over at least 60 months, starting with the month when you open your business.

Startup costs include expenses for creating an active business, investigating the creation or researching the acquisition of a business.

To qualify as a startup cost that can be amortized and included in Part V, it must meet these two tests:

- ❑ It's a cost that you could deduct if you operated an existing business.
- ❑ It's a cost that you incur before the day you open your business.

For example, expenses that would be amortized as deductible startup costs include:

- Costs of product and market research to determine the feasibility of starting a specific kind of business
- Costs related to selecting a business site
- Professional and consulting fees paid in forming your business
- Advertising for the opening of your business
- Salaries for training employees

To claim business startup amortization expenses for the first tax year you're in business, you must complete Form 4562, Depreciation and Amortization. Enter your amortization costs in Part VI of that form. Carry that amount over to Schedule C, Part V, "Other expenses."

You must also attach a statement to your Form 4562 that details your amortization costs. The statement must contain all of the following information:

- ❑ A description of the business to which the startup costs pertain
- ❑ An itemized list of each startup cost you incurred
- ❑ The month your active business began or the month you acquired the business
- ❑ The number of months in your amortization period (not less than 60)

Although you must file Form 4562 for the first year you claim amortization, you don't necessarily have to use the form in future years. In the future, if you file Form 4562 for other reasons, such as putting a capital asset into service, then continue to enter your business startup amortization in Part VI of Form 4562 and carry that amount to Schedule C, Part V. If you don't file Form 4562 in a particular year, simply show your amortization deduction in Part V of Schedule C.

Figuring your amortization is easy. First total up all the costs you paid before your business actually started. Divide that total by the length of your amortization period (60 months or longer). The result is the monthly deduction amount.

Let's take an example. You decide to open a dry cleaning store. You spend $6,000 in startup costs before you ever open the doors. That includes finding a store location, training employees, lining up suppliers, advertising your grand opening and everything else you need to launch your business. You finally open the doors on Sept. 14, 2004.

In 2004, you decide to amortize your business startup costs for a period of 60 months. Divide your total costs of startup ($6,000) by your amortization period (60 months). The result is $100. That's your monthly amortization deduction.

When you file Schedule C in 2004, you'll also complete Form 4562, Part VI. You'll carry that amount over to Part V on Schedule C. For 2004, the total will be $400. That's $100 per month, multiplied by the four months in 2004 that you operated your business.

When you file Schedule C in years after 2004, your total amortization will be $1,200. That's your monthly amortization deduction of $100 multiplied by the 12 months of the year that you operated your business. You'll report that $1,200 in Part V.

Other amortization expenses deductible in Part V

Amortization costs associated with intangible assets are reported in Part V. Examples of these include:

- Amounts you pay to acquire, register, expand, protect or defend trademarks or trade names
- Amounts you pay for research and experimentation
- Goodwill
- The cost of pollution-control facilities

Expenses NOT deductible in Part V

- Penalties or fines you pay to government agencies because you violate a law. These might include fines you pay for violating city housing codes. Truckers may incur fines for violating state maximum highway weights or air quality laws. Those fines aren't deductible in Part V.
- Charitable contributions
- Political contributions

HELPFUL IRS PUBLICATIONS

The IRS offers a library full of publications that address business expenses, tax deductions and tax planning. Here's a list of publications that might be helpful in running your business:

Publication 15, Circular E, Employer's Tax Guide

Publication 15-A, Employer's Supplemental Tax Guide

Publication 15-B, Employer's Tax Guide to Fringe Benefits

Publication 334, Tax Guide for Small Business

Publication 463, Travel, Entertainment, Gift and Car Expenses

Publication 525, Taxable and Nontaxable Income

Publication 529, Miscellaneous Deductions

Publication 535, Business Expenses

Publication 536, Net Operating Losses (NOLs) for Individuals, Estates and Trusts

Publication 538, Accounting Periods and Methods

Publication 547, Casualties, Disasters and Thefts

Publication 587, Business Use of Your Home (Including Use by Day-Care Providers)

Publication 910, Guide to Free Tax Services

Publication 925, Passive Activity and At-Risk Rules

Publication 946, How To Depreciate Property

Publication 1796, Federal Tax Products on CD-ROM, contains current tax forms, instructions and publications.

Publication 3207, Small Business Resource Guide is an interactive CD-ROM that contains information for small-business owners.

Helpful IRS Tax Forms

IRS tax forms and their line-by-line instructions are also useful. Here's a short list of forms and schedules for sole proprietors. These forms are included in the back of this book:

Form 1040, Individual Income Tax Return

Form 1040, Schedule C, Profit or Loss from Business

Form 1040, Schedule SE, Self-Employment Tax

Form 4562, Depreciation and Amortization

Form 8829, Expenses for Business Use of Your Home

Form 2106, Employee Business Expenses

Getting Publications and Forms

You can download the forms and publications you need at the IRS Web site, www.irs.gov. At the site you can also order either of the CD-ROM publications mentioned above. To order print publications, forms or the CD-ROMs by telephone, call 800-TAXFORMS (800-829-3676).

WHERE TO GET TAX HELP FROM THE IRS

Taxpayer Advocate

If you've unsuccessfully attempted to solve a problem with the IRS, contact the Taxpayer Advocate. This advocate represents the taxpayer's interests within the IRS by helping resolve problems that haven't been handled properly through standard IRS channels.

To contact a Taxpayer Advocate:

- Call the Taxpayer Advocate at 877-777-4778 or 800-829-4059
- Call the IRS at 800-826-1040

or

- Complete IRS Form 911, Application for Taxpayer Assistance Order, which can then be sent to the Advocate.

For more information see IRS *Publication 1546, The Taxpayer Advocate Service of the IRS.*

IRS Online

You can access the IRS online at www.irs.gov.

The Web site has areas of special interest for small-business owners and self-employed individuals. You can also download forms, instructions and publications.

IRS By Phone

- To ask tax questions: 800-829-1040

- To order forms, instructions or publications: 800-826-3676

- To listen to pre-recorded messages covering various tax topics, including the status of your refund: 800-829-4477

IRS TaxFax Service

You can receive forms and instructions by calling (703) 368-9694 from your fax machine and following the prompts.

IRS e-file

You can file your taxes online for fast payment and to easily authorize an electronic withdrawal by the IRS or a refund deposit. Plus, the IRS sends an official acknowledgement that your return was received. For more information, visit www.irs.gov/efile.

NASE RESOURCES

National Association for the Self-Employed

The National Association for the Self-Employed (NASE) is the nation's leading resource for the self-employed and micro business owner.

The association offers a wealth of tax, financial, management and marketing information to its members through a collection of publications, Web sites and micro-business consultants.

These resources are free and easily accessible online.

NASE TaxTalk

CPAs with concentrated experience with small and micro-business tax issues give you specific answers to your personal tax questions. The answers to your specific questions are posted on a private secured server available to you 24 hours a day from anywhere in the world. Ask follow-up questions at any time, and there is no limit to the number of questions you can ask. You will get accurate answers – for free. Just go to www.NASE.org and click on TaxTalk.

TaxCentral

This is a one-stop tax resource for self employed individuals and micro-business owners. Sign up for tax reminders personalized for your business and never miss a tax deadline. Use the interactive calculators to help you complete Schedule C and other tax forms. Plus get tax tips to help reduce your tax liability. Just log on to MyNASE and enter the QuickLink TaxCentral.

ABCs of Finance

Get quick knowledgeable answers from experienced consultants who respond to your questions at ABCs of Finance. These professionals bring years of experience in public accounting and as Controllers, Chief Financial Officers and Treasurers. Their expertise is centered on supplying the self-employed and small business owner with an understanding of accounting and financial issues in today's world. Visit www.NASE.org and click on ABCs of Finance.

ShopTalk 800

Got questions about starting, managing and growing your micro-business? The micro-business consultants at NASE ShopTalk 800 have answers. These professionals have helped more than 70,000 NASE members get accurate answers to micro-business questions. Put these specialists to work for your business. You can get advice on any topic – for free. The ShopTalk 800 consultants will answer your question by e-mail or on the phone. Go to www.NASE.org or call 800-232-NASE to find out more.

EstateTalk

Many individuals think that only the very wealthy need wills, trusts, guardians and administrators. In reality, almost everyone can benefit from a will and an estate plan. At no cost to you, a licensed attorney will answer your questions on the process of will and estate planning online. Visit www.NASE.org.

Legislative Action Center

All the important legislative news you need, without the "Washington Spin." The NASE Legislative Action Center is your window on Washington. Find out how your legislators vote on micro-business legislation. Read in-depth reports about issues that impact your micro-business. Easily send letters and emails to your Members of Congress. Click on the "Advocacy" tab at www.NASE.org or go directly to http://advocacy.NASE.org.

Free E-Newsletters

Get accurate, up-to-date information for your micro-business. The NASE publishes these e-newsletters, conveniently delivered to your inbox – for free.

TaxTalk E-Letter

Insights and answers on micro-business tax topics. Delivered once a month.
Go to www.NASE.org/taxletter/asp.

Get Connected E-Letter

Tools, tips and training for micro-business owners delivered twice a month.
Go to www.EntrepreneurialConnection.com/signup.asp.

Washington Watch E-Mail Update

The latest news about legislation and regulations that impact your micro-business.
Go to http://advocacy.NASE.org.

Micro-Business Edge

Get answers to questions that are crucial to the success of your micro-business. Check back every week for fresh ideas on taxes, financing, marketing, management and more. Read more at www.NASE.org/reference/microbusiness.asp.

Trend Alerts

Hear the buzz on micro-business trends every month. And see what actions you need to take to stay ahead of the curve. Just go to www.EntrepreneurialConnection.com. Click on the "Trend Alert" tab at the top of the page.

Resource Articles

Self-Employed magazine

This print publication of the NASE is available online. Read in-depth business articles geared toward self-employed individuals and micro-business owners. Go to www.NASE.org.

www.EntrepreneurialConnection.com

The Web site delivers in-depth Success Skills Seminars on a variety of micro-business topics. The seminars are free, and new topics are posted every month. Go to www.EntrepreneurialConnecton.com and click on the "Success Skills Seminars" tab at the top of the page. Here are just a few of the seminars online now:

- Tax Strategies for Startups
- Business Resources to the Rescue
- How to Write a Winning business Plan
- Is a Low-Cost Franchise in Your Future?
- Create a Marketing Plan That Works
- Start Me Up: 10 Things You Gotta Have to Start a Business
- The Need For A Niche
- What To Do When The Entrepreneurial Thrill Is Gone

For Members Only

When you become a member of the NASE, you can sign up for a free NASE Web account. The account gives you a free e-mail address, access to the Members Only Benefits area and much more. Find out more at www.NASE.org, or call 800-232-NASE.

INDEX

I

Improvements 53, 58, 78, 82
Independent contractor 18, 29, 30, 31, 46, 69
Indirect expenses 75, 77, 78, 79
Insurance 14, 24, 35, 36, 37–39, 50, 78, 87, 101
Interest 16, 25, 31, 39–44, 52, 75, 76, 78, 87, 100, 107
Inventory 5, 29, 37, 55, 89, 90, 93
Investment risk 86–88

L

Lease 2, 24, 25, 28, 36, 37, 47, 49–52
Legal and professional services 29, 37, 44–46, 70
Legal services 45
Licenses 56–59
Listed property 32, 35
Loans 14, 25, 39, 40, 41–42, 45, 75, 87

M

Marketing materials 20, 22
Materials and supplies 55, 92
Meals 21, 22, 26, 27, 50, 59–66, 67
Merchant fees 101
Mortgage interest 40, 41, 43, 75, 76, 78

N

NAICS code 8
NASE iii–iv, 109–112
Net loss 5, 86, 105
Net profit 5, 86, 105

O

Office expense 20, 29, 46, 47, 55, 56
Office supplies 54, 92
Online advertising 19
Ordinary and necessary business expenses 1, 2, 38, 44, 60, 62, 64

P

Penalties and fines 101, 103
Pension and profit-sharing plans 28, 36, 48–49, 68
Personal property tax 57
Postage 18, 20, 101
Professional services 29, 37, 44–46, 70
Promotions 21–22
Public relations 20–21

R

Real estate taxes 58, 75, 76
Record keeping 2, 67
Reimbursed employee expenses 67–68
Rent 22, 25, 26, 27, 28, 36, 47, 49–52, 79
Repairs and maintenance 53–54
Returns and allowances 15

S

Sales taxes 57–58
Schedule SE 86, 106
Section 179 expense deduction 5, 18, 32, 33, 34–35, 36, 47, 48, 55, 56
SEP (Simplified Employee Pension) 36, 48
Shipping 20, 22, 29, 101
SIMPLE (Savings Incentive Match Plan for Employees) 36, 48

Social Security number (SSN) 7, 9, 72
Standard mileage rate 5, 23, 24, 26, 33, 39, 50, 57, 98
State unemployment taxes 56
Supplies 10, 19, 47, 53, 54–56, 92

T

Taxes 34, 39, 40, 43, 51, 54, 56, 57, 58, 59, 68, 75, 76, 89, 108
Taxes and licenses 29, 56–59
Tax credit 49, 59, 68
Tax services 45–46, 105
Telephone 33, 47, 56, 79, 101, 106
Tentative profit 5, 70, 74
Trade shows 22
Travel 21, 22, 25, 26, 27, 44, 46, 50, 59–66, 67, 105

U

Utilities 36, 47, 58, 66, 75, 79

W

Wages 22, 28, 29, 30, 31, 36, 37, 44, 56, 67–69, 91
Worker's compensation 38

IRS FORMS

Form 1040, Individual Income Tax Return

Form 1040, Schedule C, Profit or Loss from Business

Form 1040, Schedule SE, Self-Employment Tax

Form 4562, Depreciation and Amortization

Form 8829, Expenses for Business Use of Your Home

Form 2106, Employee Business Expenses

Form **1040**

Department of the Treasury—Internal Revenue Service

U.S. Individual Income Tax Return 2004 (99) IRS Use Only—Do not write or staple in this space.

For the year Jan. 1–Dec. 31, 2004, or other tax year beginning , 2004, ending , 20

OMB No. 1545-0074

Label

(See instructions on page 16.)

Use the IRS label. Otherwise, please print or type.

Presidential Election Campaign
(See page 16.)

Your first name and initial | Last name | **Your social security number**

If a joint return, spouse's first name and initial | Last name | **Spouse's social security number**

Home address (number and street). If you have a P.O. box, see page 16. | Apt. no.

City, town or post office, state, and ZIP code. If you have a foreign address, see page 16.

▲ **Important!** ▲

You **must** enter your SSN(s) above.

Note. Checking "Yes" will not change your tax or reduce your refund.

Do you, or your spouse if filing a joint return, want $3 to go to this fund? . . . ▶

	You		Spouse
	☐ Yes ☐ No		☐ Yes ☐ No

Filing Status

Check only one box.

1 ☐ Single
2 ☐ Married filing jointly (even if only one had income)
3 ☐ Married filing separately. Enter spouse's SSN above and full name here. ▶
4 ☐ Head of household (with qualifying person). (See page 17.) If the qualifying person is a child but not your dependent, enter this child's name here. ▶
5 ☐ Qualifying widow(er) with dependent child (see page 17)

Exemptions

6a ☐ **Yourself.** If someone can claim you as a dependent, **do not** check box 6a . . . .
b ☐ **Spouse** . . . .
c Dependents:

(1) First name Last name	(2) Dependent's social security number	(3) Dependent's relationship to you	(4)✓ if qualifying child for child tax credit (see page 18)
			☐
			☐
			☐
			☐

If more than four dependents, see page 18.

d Total number of exemptions claimed . . . .

Boxes checked on 6a and 6b _____
No. of children on 6c who:
● lived with you _____
● did not live with you due to divorce or separation (see page 18) _____
Dependents on 6c not entered above _____
Add numbers on lines above ▶ ☐

Income

Attach Form(s) W-2 here. Also attach Forms W-2G and 1099-R if tax was withheld.

If you did not get a W-2, see page 19.

Enclose, but do not attach, any payment. Also, please use **Form 1040-V.**

7	Wages, salaries, tips, etc. Attach Form(s) W-2	7
8a	**Taxable** interest. Attach Schedule B if required	8a
b	**Tax-exempt** interest. **Do not** include on line 8a . . .	8b
9a	Ordinary dividends. Attach Schedule B if required	9a
b	Qualified dividends (see page 20)	9b
10	Taxable refunds, credits, or offsets of state and local income taxes (see page 20) . .	10
11	Alimony received	11
12	Business income or (loss). Attach Schedule C or C-EZ	12
13	Capital gain or (loss). Attach Schedule D if required. If not required, check here ▶ ☐	13
14	Other gains or (losses). Attach Form 4797	14
15a	IRA distributions . .	15a	b Taxable amount (see page 22)	15b
16a	Pensions and annuities	16a	b Taxable amount (see page 22)	16b
17	Rental real estate, royalties, partnerships, S corporations, trusts, etc. Attach Schedule E	17
18	Farm income or (loss). Attach Schedule F	18
19	Unemployment compensation	19
20a	Social security benefits .	20a	b Taxable amount (see page 24)	20b
21	Other income. List type and amount (see page 24) _____	21
22	Add the amounts in the far right column for lines 7 through 21. This is your **total income** ▶	22

Adjusted Gross Income

23	Educator expenses (see page 26)	23
24	Certain business expenses of reservists, performing artists, and fee-basis government officials. Attach Form 2106 or 2106-EZ	24
25	IRA deduction (see page 26)	25
26	Student loan interest deduction (see page 28)	26
27	Tuition and fees deduction (see page 29)	27
28	Health savings account deduction. Attach Form 8889 .	28
29	Moving expenses. Attach Form 3903	29
30	One-half of self-employment tax. Attach Schedule SE . .	30
31	Self-employed health insurance deduction (see page 30)	31
32	Self-employed SEP, SIMPLE, and qualified plans . . .	32
33	Penalty on early withdrawal of savings	33
34a	Alimony paid **b** Recipient's SSN ▶ _____	34a
35	Add lines 23 through 34a	35
36	Subtract line 35 from line 22. This is your **adjusted gross income** . . . . . ▶	36

For Disclosure, Privacy Act, and Paperwork Reduction Act Notice, see page 75.

Cat. No. 11320B

Form **1040** (2004)

Tax and Credits	37	Amount from line 36 (adjusted gross income)	37	
	38a	Check if: ⎰ ☐ **You** were born before January 2, 1940, ☐ Blind. ⎱ Total boxes ⎱ ☐ **Spouse** was born before January 2, 1940, ☐ Blind. ⎰ checked ▶	38a	
	b	If your spouse itemizes on a separate return or you were a dual-status alien, see page 31 and check here ▶ 38b ☐		
Standard Deduction for—	39	**Itemized deductions** (from Schedule A) **or** your **standard deduction** (see left margin) . .	39	
	40	Subtract line 39 from line 37	40	
• People who checked any box on line 38a or 38b **or** who can be claimed as a dependent, see page 31.	41	If line 37 is $107,025 or less, multiply $3,100 by the total number of exemptions claimed on line 6d. If line 37 is over $107,025, see the worksheet on page 33	41	
	42	**Taxable income.** Subtract line 41 from line 40. If line 41 is more than line 40, enter -0-	42	
	43	**Tax** (see page 33). Check if any tax is from: **a** ☐ Form(s) 8814 **b** ☐ Form 4972 . . .	43	
	44	**Alternative minimum tax** (see page 35). Attach Form 6251	44	
• All others:	45	Add lines 43 and 44 . . . . ▶	45	
Single or Married filing separately, $4,850	46	Foreign tax credit. Attach Form 1116 if required . . .	46	
	47	Credit for child and dependent care expenses. Attach Form 2441	47	
	48	Credit for the elderly or the disabled. Attach Schedule R .	48	
Married filing jointly or Qualifying widow(er), $9,700	49	Education credits. Attach Form 8863	49	
	50	Retirement savings contributions credit. Attach Form 8880 . .	50	
	51	Child tax credit (see page 37)	51	
	52	Adoption credit. Attach Form 8839	52	
Head of household, $7,150	53	Credits from: **a** ☐ Form 8396 **b** ☐ Form 8859 .	53	
	54	Other credits. Check applicable box(es): **a** ☐ Form 3800 **b** ☐ Form 8801 **c** ☐ Specify _____ . .	54	
	55	Add lines 46 through 54. These are your **total credits**	55	
	56	Subtract line 55 from line 45. If line 55 is more than line 45, enter -0- . . . . . ▶	56	
Other Taxes	57	Self-employment tax. Attach Schedule SE	57	
	58	Social security and Medicare tax on tip income not reported to employer. Attach Form 4137 . .	58	
	59	Additional tax on IRAs, other qualified retirement plans, etc. Attach Form 5329 if required .	59	
	60	Advance earned income credit payments from Form(s) W-2	60	
	61	Household employment taxes. Attach Schedule H	61	
	62	Add lines 56 through 61. This is your **total tax** . . . . ▶	62	
Payments	63	Federal income tax withheld from Forms W-2 and 1099 . .	63	
	64	2004 estimated tax payments and amount applied from 2003 return	64	
If you have a qualifying child, attach Schedule EIC.	65a	**Earned income credit (EIC)**	65a	
	b	Nontaxable combat pay election ▶	65b	
	66	Excess social security and tier 1 RRTA tax withheld (see page 54)	66	
	67	Additional child tax credit. Attach Form 8812	67	
	68	Amount paid with request for extension to file (see page 54)	68	
	69	Other payments from: **a** ☐ Form 2439 **b** ☐ Form 4136 **c** ☐ Form 8885 .	69	
	70	Add lines 63, 64, 65a, and 66 through 69. These are your **total payments** . . . . ▶	70	
Refund	71	If line 70 is more than line 62, subtract line 62 from line 70. This is the amount you **overpaid**	71	
Direct deposit? See page 54 and fill in 72b, 72c, and 72d.	72a	Amount of line 71 you want **refunded to you** . . . . ▶	72a	
	▶ b	Routing number ☐☐☐☐☐☐☐☐☐ ▶ **c** Type: ☐ Checking ☐ Savings		
	▶ d	Account number ☐☐☐☐☐☐☐☐☐☐☐☐☐☐☐☐☐		
	73	Amount of line 71 you want **applied to your 2005 estimated tax** ▶	73	
Amount You Owe	74	**Amount you owe.** Subtract line 70 from line 62. For details on how to pay, see page 55 ▶	74	
	75	Estimated tax penalty (see page 55)	75	

Third Party Designee

Do you want to allow another person to discuss this return with the IRS (see page 56)? ☐ **Yes.** Complete the following. ☐ **No**

Designee's name ▶	Phone no. ▶ ( )	Personal identification number (PIN) ▶ ☐☐☐☐☐

Sign Here

Under penalties of perjury, I declare that I have examined this return and accompanying schedules and statements, and to the best of my knowledge and belief, they are true, correct, and complete. Declaration of preparer (other than taxpayer) is based on all information of which preparer has any knowledge.

Joint return? See page 17.

Keep a copy for your records.

Your signature	Date	Your occupation	Daytime phone number ( )
Spouse's signature. If a joint return, **both** must sign.	Date	Spouse's occupation	

Paid Preparer's Use Only

Preparer's signature ▶	Date	Check if self-employed ☐	Preparer's SSN or PTIN
Firm's name (or yours if self-employed), address, and ZIP code ▶		EIN	
		Phone no. ( )	

Form **1040** (2004)

SCHEDULE C
(Form 1040)

Department of the Treasury
Internal Revenue Service

Profit or Loss From Business
(Sole Proprietorship)

▶ Partnerships, joint ventures, etc., must file Form 1065 or 1065-B.

▶ Attach to Form 1040 or 1041. ▶ See Instructions for Schedule C (Form 1040).

OMB No. 1545-0074

2004

Attachment
Sequence No. **09**

Name of proprietor

Social security number (SSN)

A Principal business or profession, including product or service (see page C-2 of the instructions)

B Enter code from pages C-7, 8, & 9
▶

C Business name. If no separate business name, leave blank.

D Employer ID number (EIN), if any

E Business address (including suite or room no.) ▶ ....
City, town or post office, state, and ZIP code

F Accounting method: **(1)** ☐ Cash **(2)** ☐ Accrual **(3)** ☐ Other (specify) ▶ ....

G Did you "materially participate" in the operation of this business during 2004? If "No," see page C-3 for limit on losses   ☐ Yes ☐ No

H If you started or acquired this business during 2004, check here . . . . ▶ ☐

Part I — Income

1	Gross receipts or sales. **Caution.** If this income was reported to you on Form W-2 and the "Statutory employee" box on that form was checked, see page C-3 and check here . . . . . ▶ ☐	1	
2	Returns and allowances	2	
3	Subtract line 2 from line 1	3	
4	Cost of goods sold (from line 42 on page 2)	4	
5	**Gross profit.** Subtract line 4 from line 3	5	
6	Other income, including Federal and state gasoline or fuel tax credit or refund (see page C-3) . . .	6	
7	**Gross income.** Add lines 5 and 6 . . . . ▶	7	

Part II — Expenses. Enter expenses for business use of your home **only** on line 30.

8	Advertising	8		19	Pension and profit-sharing plans	19	
9	Car and truck expenses (see page C-3)	9		20	Rent or lease (see page C-5):		
10	Commissions and fees . .	10			**a** Vehicles, machinery, and equipment .	20a	
11	Contract labor (see page C-4)	11			**b** Other business property . . .	20b	
12	Depletion	12		21	Repairs and maintenance . .	21	
13	Depreciation and section 179 expense deduction (not included in Part III) (see page C-4)	13		22	Supplies (not included in Part III)	22	
				23	Taxes and licenses . . .	23	
				24	Travel, meals, and entertainment:		
					a Travel	24a	
14	Employee benefit programs (other than on line 19) . .	14			**b** Meals and entertainment		
15	Insurance (other than health) .	15			**c** Enter nondeductible amount included on line 24b (see page C-5)		
16	Interest:						
	a Mortgage (paid to banks, etc.) .	16a			**d** Subtract line 24c from line 24b .	24d	
	b Other	16b		25	Utilities	25	
17	Legal and professional services	17		26	Wages (less employment credits) .	26	
18	Office expense	18		27	Other expenses (from line 48 on page 2)	27	

28	**Total expenses** before expenses for business use of home. Add lines 8 through 27 in columns . ▶	28	
29	Tentative profit (loss). Subtract line 28 from line 7	29	
30	Expenses for business use of your home. Attach **Form 8829**	30	
31	**Net profit or (loss).** Subtract line 30 from line 29. • If a profit, enter on **Form 1040, line 12,** and **also** on **Schedule SE, line 2** (statutory employees, see page C-6). Estates and trusts, enter on Form 1041, line 3. • If a loss, you **must** go to line 32.	31	

32 If you have a loss, check the box that describes your investment in this activity (see page C-6).

• If you checked 32a, enter the loss on **Form 1040, line 12,** and **also** on **Schedule SE, line 2** (statutory employees, see page C-6). Estates and trusts, enter on Form 1041, line 3.

• If you checked 32b, you **must** attach **Form 6198.**

32a ☐ All investment is at risk.

32b ☐ Some investment is not at risk.

For Paperwork Reduction Act Notice, see Form 1040 instructions.   Cat. No. 11334P   Schedule C (Form 1040) 2004

Part III   **Cost of Goods Sold** (see page C-6)

33   Method(s) used to
value closing inventory: **a** ☐ Cost   **b** ☐ Lower of cost or market   **c** ☐ Other (attach explanation)

34   Was there any change in determining quantities, costs, or valuations between opening and closing inventory? If
"Yes," attach explanation . . . . ☐ **Yes**   ☐ **No**

35	Inventory at beginning of year. If different from last year's closing inventory, attach explanation . .	**35**	
36	Purchases less cost of items withdrawn for personal use	**36**	
37	Cost of labor. Do not include any amounts paid to yourself	**37**	
38	Materials and supplies	**38**	
39	Other costs	**39**	
40	Add lines 35 through 39	**40**	
41	Inventory at end of year	**41**	
42	**Cost of goods sold.** Subtract line 41 from line 40. Enter the result here and on page 1, line 4 . .	**42**	

Part IV   **Information on Your Vehicle. Complete this part only if you are claiming car or truck expenses on
line 9 and are not required to file Form 4562 for this business. See the instructions for line 13 on page
C-4 to find out if you must file Form 4562.**

43   When did you place your vehicle in service for business purposes? (month, day, year) ▶ ..../.........../........ .

44   Of the total number of miles you drove your vehicle during 2004, enter the number of miles you used your vehicle for:

   a   Business ....   **b** Commuting ....   **c** Other ....

45   Do you (or your spouse) have another vehicle available for personal use?. . . . . ☐ **Yes**   ☐ **No**

46   Was your vehicle available for personal use during off-duty hours? . . . . ☐ **Yes**   ☐ **No**

47a   Do you have evidence to support your deduction? . . . . ☐ **Yes**   ☐ **No**

   b   If "Yes," is the evidence written? . . . . ☐ **Yes**   ☐ **No**

Part V   **Other Expenses. List below business expenses not included on lines 8–26 or line 30.**

48	**Total other expenses.** Enter here and on page 1, line 27	**48**	

SCHEDULE SE		Self-Employment Tax	OMB No. 1545-0074
(Form 1040)			**20**04
Department of the Treasury Internal Revenue Service		▶ **Attach to Form 1040.** ▶ **See Instructions for Schedule SE (Form 1040).**	Attachment Sequence No. **17**

Name of person with **self-employment** income (as shown on Form 1040)	Social security number of person with **self-employment** income ▶	

Who Must File Schedule SE

You must file Schedule SE if:

- You had net earnings from self-employment from **other than** church employee income (line 4 of Short Schedule SE or line 4c of Long Schedule SE) of $400 or more **or**
- You had church employee income of $108.28 or more. Income from services you performed as a minister or a member of a religious order **is not** church employee income (see page SE-1).

Note. Even if you had a loss or a small amount of income from self-employment, it may be to your benefit to file Schedule SE and use either "optional method" in Part II of Long Schedule SE (see page SE-3).

Exception. If your only self-employment income was from earnings as a minister, member of a religious order, or Christian Science practitioner **and** you filed Form 4361 and received IRS approval not to be taxed on those earnings, **do not** file Schedule SE. Instead, write "Exempt–Form 4361" on Form 1040, line 57.

May I Use Short Schedule SE or Must I Use Long Schedule SE?

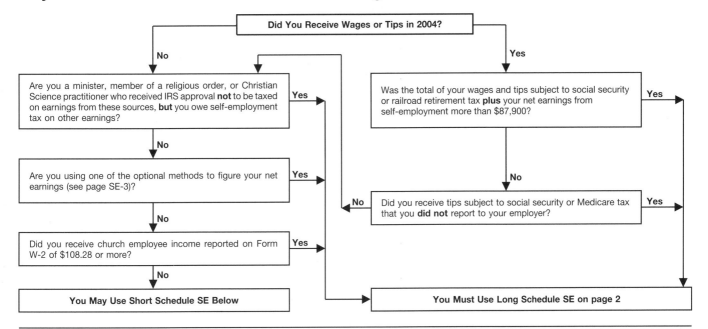

Section A—Short Schedule SE. Caution. Read above to see if you can use Short Schedule SE.

1	Net farm profit or (loss) from Schedule F, line 36, and farm partnerships, Schedule K-1 (Form 1065), box 14, code A	**1**	
2	Net profit or (loss) from Schedule C, line 31; Schedule C-EZ, line 3; Schedule K-1 (Form 1065), box 14, code A (other than farming); and Schedule K-1 (Form 1065-B), box 9. Ministers and members of religious orders, see page SE-1 for amounts to report on this line. See page SE-2 for other income to report	**2**	
3	Combine lines 1 and 2	**3**	
4	**Net earnings from self-employment.** Multiply line 3 by 92.35% (.9235). If less than $400, **do not** file this schedule; you do not owe self-employment tax . . . . . . ▶	**4**	
5	**Self-employment tax.** If the amount on line 4 is: • $87,900 or less, multiply line 4 by 15.3% (.153). Enter the result here and on **Form 1040, line 57.** • More than $87,900, multiply line 4 by 2.9% (.029). Then, add $10,899.60 to the result. Enter the total here and on **Form 1040, line 57.**	**5**	
6	**Deduction for one-half of self-employment tax.** Multiply line 5 by 50% (.5). Enter the result here and on **Form 1040, line 30**	**6**	

For Paperwork Reduction Act Notice, see Form 1040 instructions.   Cat. No. 11358Z   **Schedule SE (Form 1040) 2004**

Name of person with **self-employment** income (as shown on Form 1040)	Social security number of person with **self-employment** income ▶			

Section B—Long Schedule SE

Part I   Self-Employment Tax

Note. If your only income subject to self-employment tax is **church employee income,** skip lines 1 through 4b. Enter -0- on line 4c and go to line 5a. Income from services you performed as a minister or a member of a religious order **is not** church employee income. See page SE-1.

A   If you are a minister, member of a religious order, or Christian Science practitioner **and** you filed Form 4361, but you had $400 or more of **other** net earnings from self-employment, check here and continue with Part I . . . . . . ▶ ☐

1	Net farm profit or (loss) from Schedule F, line 36, and farm partnerships, Schedule K-1 (Form 1065), box 14, code A. **Note.** Skip this line if you use the farm optional method (see page SE-4)	**1**	
2	Net profit or (loss) from Schedule C, line 31; Schedule C-EZ, line 3; Schedule K-1 (Form 1065), box 14, code A (other than farming); and Schedule K-1 (Form 1065-B), box 9. Ministers and members of religious orders, see page SE-1 for amounts to report on this line. See page SE-2 for other income to report. **Note.** Skip this line if you use the nonfarm optional method (see page SE-4)	**2**	
3	Combine lines 1 and 2	**3**	
4a	If line 3 is more than zero, multiply line 3 by 92.35% (.9235). Otherwise, enter amount from line 3	**4a**	
b	If you elect one or both of the optional methods, enter the total of lines 15 and 17 here . . .	**4b**	
c	Combine lines 4a and 4b. If less than $400, **stop;** you do not owe self-employment tax. **Exception.** If less than $400 and you had **church employee income,** enter -0- and continue. . . . . . ▶	**4c**	

5a	Enter your **church employee income** from Form W-2. See page SE-1 for definition of church employee income	**5a**	
b	Multiply line 5a by 92.35% (.9235). If less than $100, enter -0-	**5b**	
6	**Net earnings from self-employment.** Add lines 4c and 5b	**6**	
7	Maximum amount of combined wages and self-employment earnings subject to social security tax or the 6.2% portion of the 7.65% railroad retirement (tier 1) tax for 2004	**7**	87,900 00
8a	Total social security wages and tips (total of boxes 3 and 7 on Form(s) W-2) and railroad retirement (tier 1) compensation. If $87,900 or more, skip lines 8b through 10, and go to line 11	**8a**	
b	Unreported tips subject to social security tax (from Form 4137, line 9)	**8b**	
c	Add lines 8a and 8b	**8c**	
9	Subtract line 8c from line 7. If zero or less, enter -0- here and on line 10 and go to line 11 . ▶	**9**	
10	Multiply the **smaller** of line 6 or line 9 by 12.4% (.124)	**10**	
11	Multiply line 6 by 2.9% (.029)	**11**	
12	**Self-employment tax.** Add lines 10 and 11. Enter here and on **Form 1040, line 57** . . .	**12**	
13	**Deduction for one-half of self-employment tax.** Multiply line 12 by 50% (.5). Enter the result here and on **Form 1040, line 30**	**13**	

Part II   Optional Methods To Figure Net Earnings (see page SE-3)

Farm Optional Method. You may use this method **only** if **(a)** your gross farm income[1] was not more than $2,400 **or (b)** your net farm profits[2] were less than $1,733.

14	Maximum income for optional methods	**14**	1,600 00
15	Enter the **smaller** of: two-thirds (⅔) of gross farm income[1] (not less than zero) **or** $1,600. Also include this amount on line 4b above	**15**	

Nonfarm Optional Method. You may use this method **only** if **(a)** your net nonfarm profits[3] were less than $1,733 and also less than 72.189% of your gross nonfarm income[4] **and (b)** you had net earnings from self-employment of at least $400 in 2 of the prior 3 years.

Caution. You may use this method no more than five times.

16	Subtract line 15 from line 14	**16**	
17	Enter the **smaller** of: two-thirds (⅔) of gross nonfarm income[4] (not less than zero) **or** the amount on line 16. Also include this amount on line 4b above	**17**	

[1] From Sch. F, line 11, and Sch. K-1 (Form 1065), box 14, code B.

[2] From Sch. F, line 36, and Sch. K-1 (Form 1065), box 14, code A.

[3] From Sch. C, line 31; Sch. C-EZ, line 3; Sch. K-1 (Form 1065), box 14, code A; and Sch. K-1 (Form 1065-B), box 9.

[4] From Sch. C, line 7; Sch. C-EZ, line 1; Sch. K-1 (Form 1065), box 14, code C; and Sch. K-1 (Form 1065-B), box 9.

Form **4562**	**Depreciation and Amortization** (Including Information on Listed Property)	OMB No. 1545-0172
Department of the Treasury Internal Revenue Service	▶ See separate instructions.　▶ Attach to your tax return.	**2004** Attachment Sequence No. **67**

Name(s) shown on return	Business or activity to which this form relates	Identifying number

Part I　Election To Expense Certain Property Under Section 179

Note: *If you have any listed property, complete Part V before you complete Part I.*

1	Maximum amount. See page 2 of the instructions for a higher limit for certain businesses . . .	**1** $102,000
2	Total cost of section 179 property placed in service (see page 3 of the instructions)	**2**
3	Threshold cost of section 179 property before reduction in limitation	**3** $410,000
4	Reduction in limitation. Subtract line 3 from line 2. If zero or less, enter -0-	**4**
5	Dollar limitation for tax year. Subtract line 4 from line 1. If zero or less, enter -0-. If married filing separately, see page 3 of the instructions.	**5**

(a) Description of property	(b) Cost (business use only)	(c) Elected cost
6		

7	Listed property. Enter the amount from line 29	**7**
8	Total elected cost of section 179 property. Add amounts in column (c), lines 6 and 7	**8**
9	Tentative deduction. Enter the **smaller** of line 5 or line 8.	**9**
10	Carryover of disallowed deduction from line 13 of your 2003 Form 4562	**10**
11	Business income limitation. Enter the smaller of business income (not less than zero) or line 5 (see instructions)	**11**
12	Section 179 expense deduction. Add lines 9 and 10, but do not enter more than line 11 . . .	**12**
13	Carryover of disallowed deduction to 2005. Add lines 9 and 10, less line 12 ▶	**13**

Note: *Do not use Part II or Part III below for listed property. Instead, use Part V.*

Part II　Special Depreciation Allowance and Other Depreciation (Do not include listed property.)

14	Special depreciation allowance for qualified property (other than listed property) placed in service during the tax year (see page 3 of the instructions)	**14**
15	Property subject to section 168(f)(1) election (see page 4 of the instructions)	**15**
16	Other depreciation (including ACRS) (see page 4 of the instructions)	**16**

Part III　MACRS Depreciation (Do not include listed property.) (See page 5 of the instructions.)

Section A

17	MACRS deductions for assets placed in service in tax years beginning before 2004	**17**
18	If you are electing under section 168(i)(4) to group any assets placed in service during the tax year into one or more general asset accounts, check here . . . . ▶ ☐	

Section B—Assets Placed in Service During 2004 Tax Year Using the General Depreciation System

(a) Classification of property	(b) Month and year placed in service	(c) Basis for depreciation (business/investment use only—see instructions)	(d) Recovery period	(e) Convention	(f) Method	(g) Depreciation deduction
19a 3-year property						
b 5-year property						
c 7-year property						
d 10-year property						
e 15-year property						
f 20-year property						
g 25-year property			25 yrs.		S/L	
h Residential rental property			27.5 yrs.	MM	S/L	
			27.5 yrs.	MM	S/L	
i Nonresidential real property			39 yrs.	MM	S/L	
				MM	S/L	

Section C—Assets Placed in Service During 2004 Tax Year Using the Alternative Depreciation System

(a)	(b)	(c)	(d)	(e)	(f)	(g)
20a Class life					S/L	
b 12-year			12 yrs.		S/L	
c 40-year			40 yrs.	MM	S/L	

Part IV　Summary (see page 8 of the instructions)

21	Listed property. Enter amount from line 28	**21**
22	**Total.** Add amounts from line 12, lines 14 through 17, lines 19 and 20 in column (g), and line 21. Enter here and on the appropriate lines of your return. Partnerships and S corporations—see instr.	**22**
23	For assets shown above and placed in service during the current year, enter the portion of the basis attributable to section 263A costs . .	**23**

For Paperwork Reduction Act Notice, see separate instructions.　　Cat. No. 12906N　　Form **4562** (2004)

Part V **Listed Property** (Include automobiles, certain other vehicles, cellular telephones, certain computers, and property used for entertainment, recreation, or amusement.)

Note: *For any vehicle for which you are using the standard mileage rate or deducting lease expense, complete only 24a, 24b, columns (a) through (c) of Section A, all of Section B, and Section C if applicable.*

Section A—Depreciation and Other Information (Caution: *See page 9 of the instructions for limits for passenger automobiles.***)**

24a Do you have evidence to support the business/investment use claimed? ☐ **Yes** ☐ **No** **24b** If "Yes," is the evidence written? ☐ **Yes** ☐ **No**

(a) Type of property (list vehicles first)	(b) Date placed in service	(c) Business/ investment use percentage	(d) Cost or other basis	(e) Basis for depreciation (business/investment use only)	(f) Recovery period	(g) Method/ Convention	(h) Depreciation deduction	(i) Elected section 179 cost
25 Special depreciation allowance for qualified listed property placed in service during the tax year and used more than 50% in a qualified business use (see page 8 of the instructions) **25**								
26 Property used more than 50% in a qualified business use (see page 8 of the instructions):								
		%						
		%						
		%						
27 Property used 50% or less in a qualified business use (see page 8 of the instructions):								
		%				S/L –		
		%				S/L –		
		%				S/L –		

28 Add amounts in column (h), lines 25 through 27. Enter here and on line 21, page 1. . **28**

29 Add amounts in column (i), line 26. Enter here and on line 7, page 1. . . . . **29**

Section B—Information on Use of Vehicles

Complete this section for vehicles used by a sole proprietor, partner, or other "more than 5% owner," or related person.

If you provided vehicles to your employees, first answer the questions in Section C to see if you meet an exception to completing this section for those vehicles.

		(a) Vehicle 1		(b) Vehicle 2		(c) Vehicle 3		(d) Vehicle 4		(e) Vehicle 5		(f) Vehicle 6	
30	Total business/investment miles driven during the year (**do not** include commuting miles—See page 2 of the instructions) .												
31	Total commuting miles driven during the year												
32	Total other personal (noncommuting) miles driven												
33	Total miles driven during the year. Add lines 30 through 32												
		Yes	No	Yes	No	Yes	No	Yes	No	Yes	No	Yes	No
34	Was the vehicle available for personal use during off-duty hours?.												
35	Was the vehicle used primarily by a more than 5% owner or related person?												
36	Is another vehicle available for personal use?												

Section C—Questions for Employers Who Provide Vehicles for Use by Their Employees

Answer these questions to determine if you meet an exception to completing Section B for vehicles used by employees who **are not** more than 5% owners or related persons (see page 10 of the instructions).

		Yes	No
37	Do you maintain a written policy statement that prohibits all personal use of vehicles, including commuting, by your employees?		
38	Do you maintain a written policy statement that prohibits personal use of vehicles, except commuting, by your employees? See page 10 of the instructions for vehicles used by corporate officers, directors, or 1% or more owners		
39	Do you treat all use of vehicles by employees as personal use?		
40	Do you provide more than five vehicles to your employees, obtain information from your employees about the use of the vehicles, and retain the information received?		
41	Do you meet the requirements concerning qualified automobile demonstration use? (See page 10 of the instructions.) .		

Note: *If your answer to 37, 38, 39, 40, or 41 is "Yes," do not complete Section B for the covered vehicles.*

Part VI **Amortization**

(a) Description of costs	(b) Date amortization begins	(c) Amortizable amount	(d) Code section	(e) Amortization period or percentage	(f) Amortization for this year
42 Amortization of costs that begins during your 2004 tax year (see page 11 of the instructions):					

43 Amortization of costs that began before your 2004 tax year. **43**

44 **Total.** Add amounts in column (f). See page 12 of the instructions for where to report. . . **44**

Form **8829**	**Expenses for Business Use of Your Home**	OMB No. 1545-1266
Department of the Treasury Internal Revenue Service (99)	▶ File only with Schedule C (Form 1040). Use a separate Form 8829 for each home you used for business during the year. ▶ See separate instructions.	**2004** Attachment Sequence No. **66**

Name(s) of proprietor(s)	Your social security number

Part I Part of Your Home Used for Business

1	Area used regularly and exclusively for business, regularly for day care, or for storage of inventory or product samples (see instructions)	**1**	
2	Total area of home	**2**	
3	Divide line 1 by line 2. Enter the result as a percentage	**3**	%

- For day-care facilities not used exclusively for business, also complete lines 4–6.
- All others, skip lines 4–6 and enter the amount from line 3 on line 7.

4	Multiply days used for day care during year by hours used per day	**4**		hr.
5	Total hours available for use during the year (366 days × 24 hours) (see instructions)	**5**	8,784	hr.
6	Divide line 4 by line 5. Enter the result as a decimal amount	**6**	.	
7	Business percentage. For day-care facilities not used exclusively for business, multiply line 6 by line 3 (enter the result as a percentage). All others, enter the amount from line 3 ▶	**7**		%

Part II Figure Your Allowable Deduction

8	Enter the amount from Schedule C, line 29, **plus** any net gain or (loss) derived from the business use of your home and shown on Schedule D or Form 4797. If more than one place of business, see instructions		**8**	

See instructions for columns **(a)** and **(b)** before completing lines 9–20.

		(a) Direct expenses	**(b)** Indirect expenses		
9	Casualty losses (see instructions)	**9**			
10	Deductible mortgage interest (see instructions)	**10**			
11	Real estate taxes (see instructions)	**11**			
12	Add lines 9, 10, and 11	**12**			
13	Multiply line 12, column (b) by line 7		**13**		
14	Add line 12, column (a) and line 13			**14**	
15	Subtract line 14 from line 8. If zero or less, enter -0-			**15**	
16	Excess mortgage interest (see instructions)	**16**			
17	Insurance	**17**			
18	Repairs and maintenance	**18**			
19	Utilities	**19**			
20	Other expenses (see instructions)	**20**			
21	Add lines 16 through 20	**21**			
22	Multiply line 21, column (b) by line 7		**22**		
23	Carryover of operating expenses from 2003 Form 8829, line 41		**23**		
24	Add line 21 in column (a), line 22, and line 23			**24**	
25	Allowable operating expenses. Enter the **smaller** of line 15 or line 24			**25**	
26	Limit on excess casualty losses and depreciation. Subtract line 25 from line 15			**26**	
27	Excess casualty losses (see instructions)		**27**		
28	Depreciation of your home from Part III below		**28**		
29	Carryover of excess casualty losses and depreciation from 2003 Form 8829, line 42		**29**		
30	Add lines 27 through 29			**30**	
31	Allowable excess casualty losses and depreciation. Enter the **smaller** of line 26 or line 30			**31**	
32	Add lines 14, 25, and 31			**32**	
33	Casualty loss portion, if any, from lines 14 and 31. Carry amount to **Form 4684**, Section B			**33**	
34	Allowable expenses for business use of your home. Subtract line 33 from line 32. Enter here and on Schedule C, line 30. If your home was used for more than one business, see instructions ▶			**34**	

Part III Depreciation of Your Home

35	Enter the **smaller** of your home's adjusted basis or its fair market value (see instructions)	**35**	
36	Value of land included on line 35	**36**	
37	Basis of building. Subtract line 36 from line 35	**37**	
38	Business basis of building. Multiply line 37 by line 7	**38**	
39	Depreciation percentage (see instructions)	**39**	%
40	Depreciation allowable (see instructions). Multiply line 38 by line 39. Enter here and on line 28 above	**40**	

Part IV Carryover of Unallowed Expenses to 2005

41	Operating expenses. Subtract line 25 from line 24. If less than zero, enter -0-	**41**	
42	Excess casualty losses and depreciation. Subtract line 31 from line 30. If less than zero, enter -0-	**42**	

For Paperwork Reduction Act Notice, see page 4 of separate instructions.   Cat. No. 13232M   Form **8829** (2004)

Form **2106**

Department of the Treasury
Internal Revenue Service (99)

Employee Business Expenses

▶ See separate instructions.

▶ Attach to Form 1040.

OMB No. 1545-0139

2004

Attachment
Sequence No. **54**

Your name	Occupation in which you incurred expenses	Social security number

Part I Employee Business Expenses and Reimbursements

Step 1 Enter Your Expenses

			Column A Other Than Meals and Entertainment		Column B Meals and Entertainment
1	Vehicle expense from line 22 or line 29. (Rural mail carriers: See instructions.)	**1**			
2	Parking fees, tolls, and transportation, including train, bus, etc., that **did not** involve overnight travel or commuting to and from work . .	**2**			
3	Travel expense while away from home overnight, including lodging, airplane, car rental, etc. **Do not** include meals and entertainment.	**3**			
4	Business expenses not included on lines 1 through 3. **Do not** include meals and entertainment.	**4**			
5	Meals and entertainment expenses (see instructions)	**5**			
6	**Total expenses.** In Column A, add lines 1 through 4 and enter the result. In Column B, enter the amount from line 5	**6**			

Note: *If you were not reimbursed for any expenses in Step 1, skip line 7 and enter the amount from line 6 on line 8.*

Step 2 Enter Reimbursements Received From Your Employer for Expenses Listed in Step 1

7	Enter reimbursements received from your employer that were **not** reported to you in box 1 of Form W-2. Include any reimbursements reported under code "L" in box 12 of your Form W-2 (see instructions)	**7**			

Step 3 Figure Expenses To Deduct on Schedule A (Form 1040)

8	Subtract line 7 from line 6. If zero or less, enter -0-. However, if line 7 is greater than line 6 in Column A, report the excess as income on Form 1040, line 7	**8**			
	Note: *If* **both** *columns of line 8 are zero, you cannot deduct employee business expenses. Stop here and attach Form 2106 to your return.*				
9	In Column A, enter the amount from line 8. In Column B, multiply line 8 by 50% (.50). (Employees subject to Department of Transportation (DOT) hours of service limits: Multiply meal expenses incurred while away from home on business by 70% (.70) instead of 50%. For details, see instructions.)	**9**			
10	Add the amounts on line 9 of both columns and enter the total here. **Also, enter the total on Schedule A (Form 1040), line 20.** (Reservists, qualified performing artists, fee-basis state or local government officials, and individuals with disabilities: See the instructions for special rules on where to enter the total.) . . . . ▶	**10**			

For Paperwork Reduction Act Notice, see instructions.

Cat. No. 11700N

Form **2106** (2004)

Part II   Vehicle Expenses

Section A—General Information (You must complete this section if you are claiming vehicle expenses.)

		(a) Vehicle 1	**(b)** Vehicle 2
11	Enter the date the vehicle was placed in service	11 / /	/ /
12	Total miles the vehicle was driven during 2004	12 miles	miles
13	Business miles included on line 12	13 miles	miles
14	Percent of business use. Divide line 13 by line 12	14 %	%
15	Average daily roundtrip commuting distance.	15 miles	miles
16	Commuting miles included on line 12	16 miles	miles
17	Other miles. Add lines 13 and 16 and subtract the total from line 12. . .	17 miles	miles
18	Do you (or your spouse) have another vehicle available for personal use?	☐ Yes	☐ No
19	Was your vehicle available for personal use during off-duty hours?	☐ Yes	☐ No
20	Do you have evidence to support your deduction?.	☐ Yes	☐ No
21	If "Yes," is the evidence written?.	☐ Yes	☐ No

Section B—Standard Mileage Rate (See the instructions for Part II to find out whether to complete this section or Section C.)

22	Multiply line 13 by 37.5¢ (.375)	22	

Section C—Actual Expenses

		(a) Vehicle 1		**(b)** Vehicle 2	
23	Gasoline, oil, repairs, vehicle insurance, etc.	**23**			
24a	Vehicle rentals.	**24a**			
b	Inclusion amount (see instructions) .	**24b**			
c	Subtract line 24b from line 24a .	**24c**			
25	Value of employer-provided vehicle (applies only if 100% of annual lease value was included on Form W-2—see instructions)	**25**			
26	Add lines 23, 24c, and 25 . .	**26**			
27	Multiply line 26 by the percentage on line 14 . . .	**27**			
28	Depreciation (see instructions) .	**28**			
29	Add lines 27 and 28. Enter total here and on line 1.	**29**			

Section D—Depreciation of Vehicles (Use this section only if you owned the vehicle and are completing Section C for the vehicle.)

		(a) Vehicle 1		**(b)** Vehicle 2	
30	Enter cost or other basis (see instructions)	**30**			
31	Enter section 179 deduction and special allowance (see instructions)	**31**			
32	Multiply line 30 by line 14 (see instructions if you claimed the section 179 deduction or special allowance)	**32**			
33	Enter depreciation method and percentage (see instructions) .	**33**			
34	Multiply line 32 by the percentage on line 33 (see instructions) . .	**34**			
35	Add lines 31 and 34	**35**			
36	Enter the applicable limit explained in the line 36 instructions . . .	**36**			
37	Multiply line 36 by the percentage on line 14 . . .	**37**			
38	Enter the **smaller** of line 35 or line 37. Also enter this amount on line 28 above	**38**			

SCHEDULE C
from A to Z

The Sole Proprietor's Guide to Tax Savings

Robert Hughes, CPA

National Association
for the Self-Employed

Schedule C from A to Z – The Sole Proprietor's Guide to Tax Savings

ISBN 0-9765834-0-2

Schedule C from A to Z provides information pertinent to micro-business owners and the self-employed. It is not intended to replace the role of the tax professional in your business matters. As always, it is recommended that you consult with your own business professionals for advice regarding your specific facts and circumstances.